THE ART
OF
DUTCH
COOKING

by

C. Countess van Limburg Stirum

DRAWINGS BY THE AUTHOR

HIPPOCRENE BOOKS
New York

Published by arrangement with Gramercy Publishing Company.

Hippocrene paperback edition 1998.

For information, address:
HIPPOCRENE BOOKS, INC.
171 Madison Avenue
New York, NY 10016

ISBN 0-7818-0582-1

Printed in the United States of America.

To NOJA
With many thanks

A culinary journey to Holland

CONTENTS

Recipes capitalized in the text may be located by consulting the Index.

Life has not changed so very much

PREFACE

With this little book I hope to introduce to you "how the Dutch treat" in the best sense of this so often ill used expression.

Most people have seen a painting by an old Dutch Master (either a reproduction, or the original in a museum) of a family gathered round a sumptuous meal, of village people skating on the frozen canals, or of a woman busy in her house with its floor of black and white tiles and the sun streaming in through a high window. And since those days life in my country has not changed so very much, nor has the food the people eat.

A foreigner in Holland, as a tourist, has only too little chance to share this daily, rather homely life, which centers for the greater part around the family, from the day a beautiful new baby is introduced in its long dress (a family heirloom) to the friends of its mamma, to all the fun the family has with Sint Nicolaas on the fifth of December.

The restaurants in Holland give as a rule a good sample of international cooking, for the simple reason that the Dutch people eat their national dishes in their own homes and when they go out, they want to eat something different.

I have tried in this book not only to give you Dutch recipes but also to bring you some of the atmosphere of my country, where many ancient customs have survived and live on in the family circle.

For most people, Dutch food is an undiscovered territory, and I sincerely hope that the discovery of it will bring you joy and many pleasant meals.

INTRODUCTION
TO DUTCH FOOD

Naturally every country has its own national food, depending on the climate and the products of the soil. The Russians have their caviar and vodka, the Italians their pastas and Chianti, and so on.

The Dutch have their meadows with cattle, which means milk, butter, and meat; their canals and the sea, meaning fish. Vegetables and fruit grow extremely well in this not-very-cold but rather dampish climate. The national drink is Genever, or Dutch gin.

It is not yet customary to have everything frozen or in cans and ready for use at any moment, as in America. Therefore the basis of the food is its freshness, and one could say that meals in Holland "go with the seasons." In spring the products are different and the preparation is lighter than that for food eaten in winter, which is heavier and richer.

Of course it is not possible to give a standard work on Dutch cooking, as there are so many ingredients that do not exist outside Holland, such as fresh herring or plovers' eggs, which are found by the farmer boys in the meadows during two weeks in April—the dates being fixed by the government—and are a rare and expensive delicacy.

I have tried to use only ingredients that are available in America, or the best equivalent I could find. Most food is not complicated to prepare, though perhaps entirely new for the United States, and is often cooked in advance, which makes it easier for the housewife, as she has only to reheat it.

A DAY IN HOLLAND
AND THE MEALS TAKEN

It is customary to eat a lot of bread, all kinds of bread—white, brown, black, rye, rolls with raisins, and so forth—for breakfast and for lunch. The big meal is eaten in the evening.

8 A.M.: breakfast. Most people drink endless cups of strong tea (with sugar and a little milk) with this meal. The children eat porridge—*pap*, as it is called—with white or brown sugar, all different kinds of bread with cheese, a slice of cold meat, boiled or fried eggs, and jam. And everything with plenty of butter. Quite a meal to start the day!

10:30 A.M. Coffee with sugar and hot milk. Usually *koekjes* (cookies), or various biscuits baked at home or bought in a bakeshop, accompany the coffee. Everybody stops working. In offices, coffee is handed round at the desks; in shops and workshops, people drink it at a counter or in a canteen. It is customary for housewives to make a morning call on each other, a nice occasion for a little gossiping.

12:30 P.M.: lunch. One often finds the term *Hollandse Koffietafel* on the menu of a restaurant. It means all the various kinds of bread, sliced sausage, cheese and one little warm dish (for recipes, see Luncheon Dishes chapter), fresh fruit, and endless cups of coffee.

4 P.M. Tea with cakes and biscuits.

6 P.M. If one can afford it, this is the time for a little *apéritif*, a Genever (Dutch gin). There are many different brands, but the main difference is between "old" and "young." The old is a little more oily and stronger in taste. Genever cannot be used as "gin" and does not taste well diluted with water or used to make cocktails. It is very strong and must not be taken in great quantities, but as a quick pickup it is marvelous.

6:30 P.M.: dinner. This meal usually begins with soup, made with great quantities of meat, vegetables, and so forth. Then comes fish or meat, with potatoes and lots of gravy or sauce. For dessert there is usually a pudding or a sweet made of stale bread, macaroni, or the famous *Flensjes*, very thin pancakes (for recipes, see Desserts chapter). One usually drinks beer or water with this meal. Wine is a luxury for special occasions.

Before starting on the different recipes I want to tell you about the Dutch dish that is eaten practically at all hours of the day and night and is number one on the menus of restaurants and snack bars. This may be compared with the American hamburger; however it is eaten mostly by men, who have only a short time for a little food between business hours or are "en route" the whole day in their cars. The name of this special dish is Uitsmijter, and here follows the recipe.

UITSMIJTER
For one person

Butter
2 slices white bread
Slices boiled ham or roast beef
2 eggs
1 dill pickle

Butter the bread and cover with slices of ham or roast beef—a matter of taste. Fry the eggs and put them on top of the meat. Add the dill pickle.

When one is very hungry, one can fry the bread in butter and top with the cold meat and fried eggs.

THE ART OF DUTCH COOKING

or HOW THE DUTCH TREAT

Cheese market, Alkmaar

APPETIZERS and CHEESES

Although cheese is our national product, there exist very few original cheese dishes, like the famous Fondue in Switzerland, which is a meal in itself. Nor do we eat cheese as an after-dinner savory, as they do in England.

But as cheese is the most popular appetizer to nibble when drinking Genever, I'll tell you something about the different kinds of cheese that are made.

The three most important kinds are called after the

towns they are made in: 1) Gouda cheese, a large, flat, round cheese with a 12-inch diameter; 2) Edam cheese, a round ball, red outside (this one is well known, as it is exported all over the world); 3) Leiden cheese, the same shape as the Gouda cheese, but made with cuminseed and less fatty than the other two kinds.

The most important thing about these cheeses is their age. Some are made in spring, as soon as the cattle goes from the stables to the meadows after the winter, and is the so-called "May cheese," a very fat and creamy cheese. Some are made during the summer. They are stored for a certain time, becoming aged—more *belegen*, as they call it—and during this process they lose moisture. Therefore old cheese is much drier and sharper in taste than the young, freshly made cheese and is more expensive too. The various kinds are sold in the shops, thinly sliced or in one piece of the desired weight.

For dishes that require grated cheese, the "older" kinds are used; for sandwiches, the "younger" ones, as they are easier to slice and do not crumble. As an appetizer one uses a rather old cheese, diced and eaten with a sharp mustard.

APPETIZERS

A very nice appetizer is made in the following way.
Butter
4 slices black rye bread
3 slices creamy cheese

Butter the bread thickly and put the cheese in between, one layer on top of the other. Press between two plates so that bread and cheese adhere well together. Cut crosswise with a sharp knife.

CHEESE TRUFFLES
Kaastruffels

¼ pound butter
3 tablespoons grated cheese
Pepper, salt, celery salt, or paprika to taste
Slices stale pumpernickel, crumbled

These are very easy to make and do not need any cooking.

Cream the butter and mix with the cheese and the spices. Chill. Shape into little balls with a warm teaspoon and roll in the crumbled rye bread. Chill thoroughly and serve. Instead of rye bread, bread crumbs could be used.

STUFFED EGGS WITH CHEESE
Eieren gevuld met kaas

6   eggs
4   tablespoons butter
2   tablespoons grated Parmesan cheese
¼   teaspoon salt
¼   teaspoon pepper
½   tablespoon chopped parsley

Hard-boil the eggs. Chill and shell them. Cut them into halves lengthwise. Remove the yolks and rub them through a sieve. Melt the butter and mix with the cheese, egg yolks, salt, pepper, and parsley. Fill the eggs with this paste and chill.

MEAT BALLS
Bitterballen

3   tablespoons butter
4   tablespoons flour
1   cup milk or water
1   tablespoon very finely minced onion
1   teaspoon Worcestershire sauce
½   teaspoon grated nutmeg
½   teaspoon salt
1   tablespoon chopped parsley
1½ cups cooked, chopped meat
Bread crumbs
2   egg yolks
Fat for frying
Mustard

Melt the butter, stir in the flour, and add the milk or water. Make a thick sauce. Add the six following ingredients. Simmer for 5 minutes, stirring well. Spread this mixture on a plate, and when it is cool, shape into little balls. Roll these in the bread crumbs. Beat the egg yolks with 3 tablespoons water, roll the balls through this mixture, and see that they are covered well on all sides. Roll again through the bread crumbs. Let them stand for 1 hour; they must be dry. Drop them in hot fat, cook until they are brown, and drain them on absorbent paper. They are served with mustard, and usually it is very difficult to eat them without burning your mouth, but that is as it should be.

CHEESE CROQUETTES
Kaascroquetten

3   tablespoons butter
5   tablespoons flour
1   cup milk
1½ cups grated cheese
¼   teaspoon pepper
Sifted bread crumbs
2   egg yolks
Fat for frying

± 10 CROQUETTES OR
   20 CHEESE BALLS

Melt the butter, stir in the flour, and slowly add the milk. Cook and stir the sauce with a wire whisk until it is smooth and boiling. Add the cheese and stir until it is melted. Season with pepper. Spread on a plate and cool. Shape with a spoon into croquettes and dip them in the bread crumbs. Beat the egg yolks with 3 tablespoons water and roll the croquettes through this mixture, then again through the bread crumbs, and fry in deep fat. Drain on absorbent paper. Instead of croquettes, one can make little balls and eat these as an appetizer with a drink.

CHEESE PUFFS
Kassballetjes

3   tablespoons butter
5   tablespoons flour
1½   cups grated cheese
3   egg yolks, beaten
3   egg whites, beaten stiff
¼   teaspoon pepper
Fat for frying

± 20 PUFFS

Melt the butter, stir in the flour, and add 1 cup water. Cook and stir the sauce with a wire whisk until it is smooth and boiling. Add the cheese and stir until it is melted.

Take the sauce from the fire, add the beaten egg yolks, and fold in the egg whites. Add pepper. With a small spoon take a part of this mixture and drop into hot fat. Drain on absorbent paper.

Served with tomato sauce and a green salad, these puffs make an excellent lunch dish.

WARM CHEESE-AND-BREAD DISH
Kaas en broodschoteltje

10 slices stale bread without crusts
5 slices cheese
2 eggs
1 cup milk
1 tablespoon butter

4 SERVINGS

Place 5 slices of bread in a buttered ovenproof dish. Cover with the cheese and top with the rest of the bread. Beat the eggs with the milk and pour over the bread and cheese. Let soak for ½ hour. Dot with butter and bake in a moderate oven (350° F.) for ½ hour. Serve warm or cold. This dish goes well with a green salad.

CHEESE SOUFFLÉ
Kaas soufflé

3 tablespoons butter
2 tablespoons flour
1 cup milk
½ cup grated cheese
3 egg yolks, beaten
¼ teaspoon salt or celery salt
Pinch of pepper
3 egg whites, beaten stiff

4 SERVINGS

Melt the butter, stir in the flour, and slowly add the milk. Cook and stir the sauce with a wire whisk until it is smooth and boiling. Add the cheese and stir until it is melted. Add 3 beaten egg yolks and salt and pepper. Cool. Fold in 3 egg whites. Pour into a lightly greased baking dish, 7 inches in diameter. Bake for ½ hour in a moderate oven (350° F.), without opening the oven door to have a look. Serve at once.

I will end this chapter with a popular appetizer.

Put some shelled peanuts in a hot frying pan and shake them well. Serve with a liberal amount of salt.

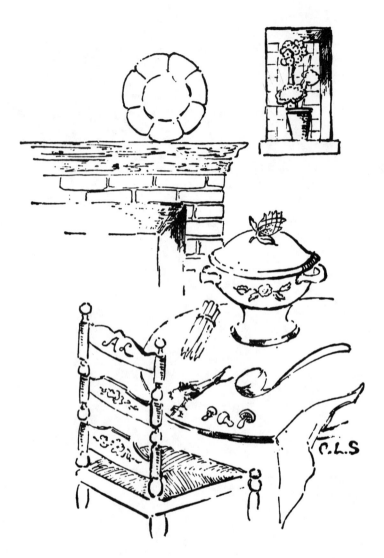

Soups

SOUPS

Soups play an important role in the Dutch cuisine, as the climate is rather damp and cold, and one likes to start a meal with something warm. Therefore cold soups are not on the national menu. Some soups, such as pea soup and bean soup, are eaten as a whole meal. They simmer the whole day over a slow fire and are eaten the next day, which improves their taste highly.

Leftover vegetables such as cauliflower or asparagus are

always used for soup too, with the water they are cooked in. So there are lots of vitamins in these soups and very few calories.

PEA SOUP
Erwtensoep

3 cups green split peas
2 pigs' feet
1-pound slab fresh bacon
3 leeks
2 onions
2 tablespoons butter
2 tablespoons chopped parsley
1 cup chopped celery stalks with leaves
1 celery root or celeriac
1 can frankfurters
Salt and pepper to taste
Pumpernickel

6 SERVINGS, AS THIS IS CONSIDERED
TO BE THE WHOLE MEAL

Cook the peas in 3 quarts water till tender, and if necessary rub them through a sieve. Add the pigs' feet and simmer for 2 hours. Add the bacon. Wash and slice the leeks and the onions. Fry them in butter and add to the soup with the parsley and celery root (cut into cubes). Simmer for 1 hour or more. Cut the frankfurters into pieces and add them with their juice to the soup. Let stand overnight. Reheat this soup the next day. Add salt and pepper. Stir well, as it will have become much thicker. Take the bacon out and cut into slices. Serve these on the pumpernickel with the soup.

From what is left of the soup make next day a

GREEN SOUP
Groene soep

Add as much water as necessary to give each person a cup.

2 tablespoons chopped parsley
Croutons fried in butter

Boil the soup, and sieve. If there is any meat left on the pigs' feet, cut this in small pieces and put back in the soup. Adjust seasoning. Fry croutons—enough for each person to add 2 spoonfuls to his cup of soup. Garnish with parsley.

BEAN SOUP
Bruine bonen soep

2   cups dried beans
1   teaspoon salt
4   whole cloves
6   peppercorns
1   bay leaf
2   leeks, sliced
¾   cup sliced celery with leaves
2   medium-sized onions, chopped
¾   cup sliced carrots
4   tablespoons fat or lard
2–3 tablespoons soya sauce
2–3 tablespoons catchup

8 SERVINGS

Soak the washed dried beans overnight in 10 cups water. Next day add to the same water the salt, cloves, peppercorns, and bay leaf. Bring to the boiling point and simmer for 4 hours. Rub through a sieve. Fry the leeks, celery, onions, and carrots in the fat. Add to the soup and simmer for 2 hours more. Before serving, add the soya sauce and the catchup. This is a spicy soup. Of course cans of beans with water added may be used.

CURRY SOUP

This is made of what is left of the Bean Soup.

        6   cups Bean Soup (water added if necessary)
        2   medium-sized onions, chopped finely
        3   tablespoons butter
        3   tablespoons flour
        1   tablespoon curry powder
        Parsley
        ¾ cup croutons fried in butter

        6 SERVINGS

Heat the Bean Soup. Fry the onions in the butter until golden brown. Blend in the flour and the curry powder. Mix well. Slowly add the soup to this mixture and cook for about 10 minutes. Rub through a sieve. Add the parsley and serve with the croutons.

MEAT BALLS,
BEEF OR VEAL, FOR SOUP
Soepballetjes

Meat balls are often added to soup. In this case it is not necessary to use meat for the stock.

      2   slices white bread without crusts,
          soaked in very little milk
      ½   pound ground fresh beef or veal
      1   egg
      ½   teaspoon salt
      ¼   teaspoon grated nutmeg

Mix all ingredients well and roll into small balls. Drop into the simmering soup and cook till done (± 10 minutes).

VEGETABLE SOUP WITH MEAT BALLS
Groentesoep met balletjes

3 cups diced fresh vegetables (leeks, carrots,
   beans, peas, parsley, celery, etc. No tomatoes)
3 tablespoons butter
1 teaspoon salt
2 tablespoons rice
Beef Meat Balls

6–8 SERVINGS

Fry the vegetables lightly in the butter and add 6 cups water, salt, and rice. Cook slightly, until they are done. Add the Beef Meat Balls, and simmer for 10 minutes.

VERMICELLI SOUP WITH MEAT BALLS
Vermicelli soep met balletjes

⅔ cup vermicelli
1 teaspoon salt
Little piece of mace
Veal Meat Balls

6 SERVINGS

Cook the vermicelli in 6 cups water with the salt and mace (this gives the extra flavor) for about ½ hour. Add the Veal Meat Balls and simmer for 10 minutes.

EEL SOUP
Paling soep

This is eaten during Lent.

1 tablespoon salt
6–8 peppercorns
½ bay leaf
1½ -pound eel, cleaned and cut into 1-inch pieces
6 tablespoons butter
6 tablespoons flour
1 tablespoon chopped parsley
2 egg yolks

8 SERVINGS

Bring 8 cups water to a boil with the salt, peppercorns, and bay leaf. Add the eel and simmer for 20 minutes. Take the eel out. Fry the butter with the flour and add the eel stock. Simmer for 15 minutes. Sieve. Add the eel and the parsley. Reheat the soup. Take the soup from the fire. Beat the egg yolks with a little of the liquid and add to the soup.

KIDNEY SOUP
Nier soep

1 veal kidney
4 cups stock or 4 cups water with 4
  bouillon cubes
1 tablespoon finely chopped onions
3 tablespoons butter
3 tablespoon flour
1 cup cream
1 small can champignons
2 tablespoons Madeira
6 SERVINGS

Soak the kidney in water for 2 hours. Change this water two or three times and cook in the stock until done (½ hour). Drain kidney and dice. Fry the onion in the butter, and add the flour. Add the cream, stirring well, and, slowly, the stock to this mixture. Simmer for 15 minutes. Then add the champignons and the diced kidney. Just before serving, stir in the Madeira.

CHERVIL SOUP
Kervel soep

5 tablespoons butter
6 tablespoons flour
6 cups veal stock
3 tablespoons chopped chervil
3 egg yolks
6–8 SERVINGS

Melt the butter and stir in the flour. Slowly add the stock. Stir well and simmer for 10 minutes. Add the chervil. Take the soup from the fire. Beat the egg yolks with a little of the liquid and add to the soup.

Hollandse Koffietafel

LUNCHEON DISHES
and recipes for leftover food as part of the
Hollandse Koffietafel

It may not sound very hospitable to give your guests a dish made of leftovers, instead of rushing to the store to buy everything fresh. But still, the best luncheon dishes are often made from refrigerator scraps. It is not the custom to have a hot meal in the middle of the day, although one luncheon dish is usually part of the *Hollandse Koffietafel.*

This last is served in the following way. All dishes are put on the table at the same time—various kinds of bread, such as white, brown, rye, pumpernickel, rolls, rusks, zwieback, and currant bread, and various kinds of meat, such as ham, liver, sausages, roast beef, etc. These are all sliced and put on separate dishes. For the children there is a variety of sweet things: jams, and an amazing assortment of sugar and chocolate products to sprinkle on the buttered slices of bread. But these are all bought ready-made. Cheese is never omitted. All this is accompanied by a seasonal salad, lettuce, tomato, or cucumber. These are prepared in a special way.

DRESSING FOR LETTUCE SALAD
Slasaus

1   hard-boiled egg
½ teaspoon salt
½ teaspoon pepper
½ teaspoon sugar
1   teaspoon mustard
3   tablespoons oil
1   tablespoon vinegar, or juice of ½ lemon
1   thin leek or spring onion, shredded

Mash the hard-boiled egg with a fork. Add salt, pepper, sugar, and mustard. Stir in the oil, vinegar or lemon juice, and the leek. The dressing should be of a smooth consistency.

The lettuce, cleaned and dried, is added gradually to this sauce in the salad bowl and thoroughly mixed.

TOMATO SALAD
Tomatensla

1 tablespoon oil
1 teaspoon salt
½ teaspoon pepper
1 teaspoon chopped onion
½ teaspoon sugar
4 tomatoes, sliced
½ tablespoon chopped parsley

Mix oil, salt, pepper, onion, and sugar. Pour this mixture over the sliced tomatoes. Sprinkle with the chopped parsley.

CUCUMBER SALAD
Komkommersla

1 cucumber
2 teaspoons salt
2 tablespoons wine vinegar
1 tablespoon chopped parsley

Peel and slice the cucumber thinly. Sprinkle with the salt and put the cucumber for 1 hour in a colander to drain off excess moisture. Add vinegar and parsley and mix well.

MACARONI WITH HAM AND CHEESE
Macaronischoteltje

1½ cups macaroni (when boiled, this
    becomes twice this amount)
1   cup chopped boiled ham
1   cup grated Parmesan cheese
3   tablespoons butter
1   tablespoon bread crumbs

3 SERVINGS

Break macaroni into 2-inch pieces. Bring to the boil in 6 cups water. Boil 15 minutes, turn off the heat, and let the macaroni stay in the water for about 15 minutes. Drain well. Add the ham, cheese, and 2 tablespoons butter. Mix, stirring with 2 spoons. Put in a greased oven-proof dish. Dot with the rest of the butter; sprinkle with the bread crumbs. Bake in a moderate hot oven (350° F.) for ½ hour.

One can vary this dish by adding sautéed chopped onions, pepper, celery salt, Worcestershire sauce, or tomato paste.

STUFFED TOMATOES
Gevulde tomaten

6   large tomatoes
½   pound meat (beef, veal, pork, or a combi-
    nation of these), ground or chopped
1   slice white bread without crust, soaked in a
    little milk
1   teaspoon grated onion
½   teaspoon salt
¼   teaspoon pepper

¼ teaspoon grated nutmeg
½ tablespoon chopped parsley
2 tablespoons butter

6 SERVINGS

Cut a slice off the top and empty each tomato with a small spoon. Keep the slices and insides for further use. Prepare the stuffing by mixing together all ingredients, except the butter. Stuff the tomatoes and put them in a greased ovenproof dish. Press a little lump of butter in each tomato. Now rub through a sieve the parts of the tomatoes you have reserved, pour this liquid between the tomatoes in the dish, and add the rest of the butter. Bake in a moderate oven (350° F.) for ½ hour.

STUFFED CUCUMBER
Gevulde komkommer

1 large cucumber
1 bouillon cube
½ pound meat (beef or veal), ground
1 slice white bread without crust, soaked in a little milk
1 teaspoon grated onion
½ teaspoon salt
¼ teaspoon pepper
¼ teaspoon grated nutmeg
2 tablespoons bread crumbs
2 tablespoons grated cheese
1 tablespoon butter

Peel and slice the cucumber lengthwise in halves and crosswise into three pieces. Take the pulp out with a spoon. Cover the six pieces with water and parboil for 8 minutes. Dissolve the bouillon cube in 1 cup of the stock. Drain the cucumber. Mix the meat with the soaked bread, onion, salt, pepper, and nutmeg. Stuff the pieces with this mixture. Put them in a greased ovenproof dish. Pour in the bouillon. Sprinkle with bread crumbs and cheese and dot with butter. Bake in a moderate oven (350° F.) for ½ hour.

HUNTERS' DISH
Jachtschotel

This dish is called Hunters' Dish because leftovers of game can be used instead of meat.

3   onions, sliced
3   tablespoons butter or fat
1   pound cooked chopped meat
Meat drippings diluted with water to make
    2 cups
½   teaspoon salt
½   teaspoon pepper
¼   teaspoon grated nutmeg
1   tablespoon Worcestershire sauce
3–4 medium-sized potatoes, mashed
4   apples, peeled and sliced very thin
1   tablespoon bread crumbs

6 SERVINGS

Sauté the onions in 2 tablespoons butter. Add the meat, liquid, and spices. Mix well. Fill a greased ovenproof dish with alternate layers of mashed potatoes, the meat-and-onion mixture, and a layer of apple slices. The top layer should be potatoes. Dot with the rest of the butter and sprinkle with bread crumbs. Bake in moderate oven (350° F.) for ½ hour.

CURRY DISH
Kerryschoteltje

3   onions, chopped
3   tablespoons butter or fat
2   teaspoons curry powder
½ teaspoon salt
1   pound cooked meat, diced
3   cups boiled rice
Meat drippings diluted with water to make
    2 cups
1   tablespoon bread crumbs

4–6 SERVINGS

Sauté the onions in 2 tablespoons butter. Stir in the curry powder and salt. Add the meat, rice, and liquid. Mix well. Put into a greased ovenproof dish and dot with the rest of the butter. Sprinkle with bread crumbs. Bake in moderate oven (350° F.) for ½ hour.

HUZARENSLA
A cold salad for Hussars

1 head lettuce (use inner leaves only)
1 pound cold cooked meat, diced
3 sour apples, diced
3 hard-boiled eggs, chopped
1 cooked beet, diced
6 boiled potatoes, mashed
4 dill pickles, sliced
4 tablespoons small pickled onions
3 tablespoons oil
3 tablespoons vinegar
Pepper and salt to taste
Mayonnaise

8 SERVINGS

Decorate an oblong dish with lettuce leaves. Mix all ingredients except the mayonnaise with the oil and vinegar and with pepper and salt. The result must be a rather solid mass. Spread this on the lettuce leaves like a pudding. Cover with a thick coating of mayonnaise.

For decoration:
2 hard-boiled eggs
Slices of dill pickle
1 tablespoon chopped parsley

Chop the whites of the eggs and rub the yolks through a sieve. Use these with round slices of the pickle and the parsley in strips or squares on top of the mayonnaise.

EGGS IN CURRY SAUCE
Eieren in kerrysaus

2 onions, chopped
4 tablespoons butter
2 teaspoons curry powder
4 tablespoons flour
1 cup milk
1 apple, diced
1 tablespoon raisins
1 teaspoon salt
8 hard-boiled eggs
1 tablespoon chopped parsley

8 SERVINGS

Sauté the onions in the butter. Add the curry powder and flour. Stir in the milk and 1 cup water and make a smooth sauce. Add the apple and simmer until the pieces are nearly dissolved. Add the raisins and salt. Slice or quarter the eggs. Put them in a dish, cover with the sauce, and sprinkle parsley on top.

Serve this dish with mango chutney, fried bananas, and rice. A cucumber salad might be served with it.

FRIED EGGS WITH CHEESE
Spiegeleieren met kaas

6 thick slices Edam cheese
3 tablespoons butter
6 eggs
Pepper or paprika

6 SERVINGS

Sauté the slices of cheese for a few minutes in butter,

turning over once. Fry the eggs in the usual manner. Put one on each slice of cheese. Sprinkle with pepper or paprika powder, depending on the taste of the cheese.

Serve with toast, butter, and a green salad. Fresh radishes go very well with this dish.

BAKED EGGS WITH ONIONS AND CHEESE
Gebakken eieren met uien en kaas

1   onion, grated
4   tablespoons butter
4   tablespoons grated cheese
6   eggs
½ cup cream

6 SERVINGS

In a shallow ovenproof dish, sauté the onion in the butter till golden brown. Sprinkle with 2 tablespoons cheese. Break the eggs over these ingredients, keeping the yolks whole. Cover with the cream and the rest of the cheese. Bake the eggs in a moderate oven (350° F.) until they are firm.

OMELETTE WITH RAGOUT
OF SHRIMPS
Omelet met garnalen ragout

4 eggs
Pinch of salt
4 tablespoons butter
2 tablespoons flour
¾ cup milk
½ cup shrimps
Pinch of grated nutmeg
½ tablespoon chopped parsley

4 SERVINGS

Beat 4 eggs with 4 tablespoons water until well blended. Add salt. In a skillet, melt 2 tablespoons butter. Add the egg mixture, cook over a slow fire, and prick with a fork until the eggs are firm. The omelette should be a delicate brown underneath.

For the ragout: Melt 2 tablespoons butter and add 2 tablespoons flour. Stir in the milk and make a smooth sauce. Add shrimps, nutmeg, and parsley. Mix well. Spread this mixture lengthwise over the middle of the omelette and fold over.

Serve with a green salad.

EGGS IN MUSTARD SAUCE
Kamper steur

This dish originates from the town of Kampen.

4 tablespoons butter
4 tablespoons flour
2 cups bouillon
1½ tablespoons mustard
1 tablespoon capers (optional)
6 hard-boiled eggs

6 SERVINGS

Melt the butter, add the flour, and stir until well blended. Stir in the bouillon and make a smooth sauce. Mix in the mustard and capers. Quarter the eggs and pour the sauce over them.

RUSSIAN EGGS (cold)
Russische eieren

2 hard-boiled eggs
Lettuce leaves
1 tablespoon sliced cucumber, marinated
1 tomato, quartered
½ tablespoon chopped parsley
½ tablespoon chopped celery stalks
Mayonnaise

1 SERVING

Cut the tops off the eggs, so that they can stand. Put them in the middle of a plate. Surround with lettuce leaves. Decorate with cucumber and tomato. Mix the parsley and the celery stalks with the mayonnaise and pour over the eggs.

Scheveningen harbor

FISH

Bordering on the North Sea, Holland has a lot of fish which is different from that of other countries. Although salmon and lobster are not on the menu, we have various other kinds of sea food that enjoy great popularity. As a rule we use only fish which is brought in fresh nearly every day and we are therefore quite dependent on the seasons. In winter, fish is rather scarce and expensive. Oysters from the Province of Zeeland (the famous Imperiales) are eaten only when there is an "R" in the name of the month beginning with SeptembeR and ending with ApRil. They are very expensive and considered a great luxury, always eaten on the half shell, on ice, with toast and butter, a little ground pepper, and a piece of lemon. To add catchup or any other sauce is considered a sacrilege. It is an old Dutch custom to consume dozens of oysters (and nothing else) on New Year's Eve, with a bottle of champagne to celebrate the coming of the New Year.

Herring—"the poor man's oyster," as it is sometimes called—is certainly a national dish and forms the basis of an important industry. Therefore the beginning of the herring season calls for some extra celebration, and the consumption of fresh, young, and fat herrings is a tradition in Holland that has no counterpart anywhere else.

On a certain date in May the herring fleet from the various seaports, such as Katwijk, Ymuiden, and Scheveningen sail out and parade along the coast for an afternoon, gaily decorated with bunting. From all over the country, people come to watch from the dunes; and, with its full sails and flags flying in the breeze, the fleet is indeed a unique sight.

When evening falls, the ships return to port, and now the serious work begins: getting ready for the big race. The skipper who brings in the first catch within twenty-four hours wins the race, and as a special honor, he is allowed to present the first herrings of the season (packed in a cask of traditional design) to Her Majesty, the Queen. His photograph appears in all the newspapers, and everybody is delighted.

And from that moment on, the whole nation eats herring—"green" herring, as it is called. The most elegant and expensive restaurants as well as the little cafés put it on their menus as a number-one specialty. The herrings are usually served on ice, with toast and butter, more or less like oysters. But the best way to eat them is from a little cart on the streets (see jacket illustration). They are decorated with the national tricolor and carry the proud announcement: *Hollandse Nieuwe* (Holland New Ones).

It is an amazing spectacle to see all classes of people flock to the herring stalls in the season: the workingman as well as the dignified businessman passing by in his car, who just cannot resist the temptation to stop and buy. But it really takes skill to eat them like this: the vendor cuts off the head, rips out the inner "works," but leaves the tail on. So take the herring between the thumb and finger of your right hand, swish it through some raw chopped onions (optional), toss your head, open your mouth—and eat (or swallow is the correct expression for this strange performance).

For the rest of the year herrings are salted or pickled in vinegar and herbs.

A salad is made of them that is rather popular in Holland and very nice as a little hors d'oeuvre to start a meal.

HERRING SALAD
Haringsla

1 head lettuce (use inner leaves only)
3 pickled herrings, chopped
3 apples, diced
3 hard-boiled eggs, chopped
2 boiled beets, diced
8 cold boiled potatoes, mashed
3 dill pickles, sliced
½ medium-sized onion, chopped very fine
Oil
Vinegar
Pepper and salt
Mayonnaise

8 SERVINGS

Decorate an oblong dish with the lettuce leaves. Mix all the ingredients with oil and vinegar, and pepper and salt to taste. The result must be a rather solid mass. Spread this on the lettuce leaves like a pudding. Cover with a thick coating of mayonnaise.

For decoration:
2 hard-boiled eggs
Slices of dill pickle
1 tablespoon chopped parsley

Chop the whites of the eggs and rub the yolks through a sieve. Use these with round slices of the pickle, and the parsley cut in strips or squares on top of the mayonnaise.

After oysters and herring, shrimps take the third place as a popular sea food. Although they are much smaller than their big American cousins, they can be eaten in the same way. In Holland they are caught fresh and eaten on slices of bread with a little lemon juice or vinegar and some pepper.

SHRIMP CROQUETTES
Garnalen croquetten

3 tablespoons butter
2½ tablespoons flour
1 cup milk
2 cups minced shrimps
1 tablespoon chopped parsley
½ teaspoon grated nutmeg
1½ cups bread crumbs
1 egg
Oil for frying

± 12 CROQUETTES

Make a thick and smooth sauce of the butter, flour, and milk. Add the shrimps, parsley, and nutmeg and stir well. Spread on a dish and let cool. Take about a heaping tablespoon of this mixture and shape in the form you wish. Roll in the bread crumbs. Beat an egg with 2 tablespoons water on a plate. Roll the croquettes through this mixture and again through the bread crumbs. The croquette must be well covered on all sides. Let them set for ½ hour. Then fry them in deep oil, at 390° F., until brown. Drain on absorbent paper. Should it be necessary to reheat them, put them for a short time in a very hot preheated oven.

SHRIMP SALAD
Garnalensla

2 cups shrimp
1 apple, diced
2 cold boiled potatoes, diced
1 tablespoon chopped celery
1 tablespoon chopped parsley
4 tablespoons oil
2 tablespoons vinegar
1 teaspoon pepper

6 SERVINGS

Mix together all ingredients and chill.

SHRIMP SAUCE
Garnalen saus

3   tablespoons butter
3   tablespoons flour
1½ cups milk or fish stock
Little piece of mace
½   tablespoon chopped parsley
1   cup shrimps
1   egg
¼   teaspoon ground pepper

Make a smooth sauce of the butter, flour, and the milk or fish stock. Add the mace, the parsley, and the shrimps. Simmer until all is blended well, but do not let the shrimps become soft. Stir in the egg and pepper. This is an excellent sauce with boiled or fried fillets of sole.

FISH CAKES
Viskoekjes

1 cup prepared fish
1 slice bread, softened in milk
1 egg
½ teaspoon salt
1 tablespoon chopped parsley
Bread crumbs
3 tablespoons butter

6 CAKES

These cakes may be made of any kind of fish or fish leftovers. Boil the fish and remove all the bones. Mince very fine. Mix all the ingredients to form cakes. Roll them through the bread crumbs and fry in butter.

BAKED FILLETS OF HADDOCK OR COD
Gestoofde kabeljauw of schelvis

4 tablespoons butter
4 tablespoons flour
2 cups milk
¼ teaspoon salt
¼ teaspoon grated nutmeg
2 egg yolks, beaten
2 egg whites, beaten stiff
6 fillets of haddock or cod
½ cup bread crumbs

6 SERVINGS

Melt the butter, add the flour, and stir in the milk. Add salt and nutmeg to this cream sauce. Take the sauce from the fire and add the egg yolks. Fold in the beaten egg whites. Put the fillets in a greased, ovenproof dish. Pour the sauce over the fish, sprinkle with the bread crumbs, and bake in a 350° F. oven for ½ hour.

Various ingredients can be added to this sauce, such as: chopped parsley, small mushrooms, shrimps, and capers. Or one can use different kinds of fish at the same time; pieces of salmon may be added to give a touch of color.

BAKED FILLETS OF HADDOCK OR COD WITH POTATOES
Gestoofde kabeljauw of schelvis met aardappelen

2   onions, chopped
3   tablespoons butter
6   fillets of haddock or cod
1   pound potatoes
3   eggs
½   teaspoon salt
1   cup sour cream
Bread crumbs

6 SERVINGS

Fry the onions in the butter. Flatten out the fish. Boil the potatoes for 10 minutes and slice them. Put in a greased ovenproof dish a layer of fish, cover with a layer of potatoes and some of the fried onions; then a layer of fish, and so forth. End with a layer of potatoes. Beat the eggs with the salt for a few minutes. Add the sour cream and pour over the fish. Sprinkle with bread crumbs and bake in a moderate oven (350° F.) for about ¾ hour. Any kind of fish can be used for this recipe.

Volendam fishermen

FRIED SOLE
Gebakken tong

4 soles (not fillets)
Salt
1 cup bread crumbs
½ cup butter
1 lemon, quartered

4 SERVINGS

Rub the soles with some salt and after ½ hour dry them thoroughly. Roll them through the bread crumbs. Brown the butter in a skillet and fry the soles on both sides till golden brown, moving them around so they don't stick to the bottom. Serve them with lemon quarters.

These may be eaten with boiled potatoes and a salad of lettuce or cucumber and melted butter.

FILLETS OF SOLE IN WHITE WINE
Tong filets in witte wijn

½ teaspoon salt
12 fillets of sole
2 cups white wine
6 tablespoons butter
3 tablespoons flour

4 SERVINGS

Salt the fillets and put them in a greased ovenproof dish. Add the wine and 3 tablespoons butter. Cover and put for 20 minutes in a moderate oven (350° F.). Fry the rest of the butter with the flour and make a sauce with the wine drained from the fish. Sieve if necessary and pour back over the fish.

FILLETS OF SOLE WITH SPINACH AND CHEESE SAUCE
Tong filets "Florentine"

12   fillets of sole
1   teaspoon salt
2½ tablespoons butter
2   cups cooked spinach
2   tablespoons flour
1   cup milk
2   tablespoons grated Parmesan cheese

4 SERVINGS

Place the fillets in boiling salted water and simmer till nearly tender. This goes quickly. Drain well and put them in a greased ovenproof dish. Cover with the spinach. Make a cream sauce of 2 tablespoons butter, the flour and the milk. Stir in the cheese and cover the spinach with the sauce. Dot with butter and put for 10 minutes in a hot oven (400° F.).

If this dish is prepared in advance, bake the fish in a moderate oven (350° F.) for ½ hour.

QUICKLY FRIED FRESH FISH

Use any kind of fillets or small, cleaned fish. Sprinkle them with salt and let stand for ½ hour. Dry and roll them 1) through flour; 2) through beaten egg; and 3) through bread crumbs. Pour enough oil in a heavy skillet so that the bottom is well covered. Heat the oil for about 4 minutes and fry the fish, turning once.

PIKE
Snoek

The trouble with pike is that there are so many small bones in it. Therefore, cut the fish open over the whole length, take out the entrails, and clean thoroughly. Now cover the fish with a mixture of ¾ vinegar and ¼ water and let stand overnight. Most of the very small bones will be dissolved.

PIKE WITH WHITE-WINE SAUCE
Snoek in witte wijn saus

1   pike of about 4 pounds
¼   cup and 4 tablespoons butter
1   tablespoon chopped parsley
1   medium-sized onion, chopped
1   tablespoon chopped celery
1   teaspoon salt
¼   teaspoon pepper
¼   teaspoon grated nutmeg
¼   teaspoon mace
1   cup white wine
Bread crumbs
1   lemon, sliced
4   tablespoons flour
1   tablespoon capers
2   egg yolks, beaten

8 SERVINGS

Cut the cleaned pike (see rule for cleaning under Pike) in pieces and arrange these in the original shape of the fish in a greased ovenproof dish. Fry in ¼ cup butter the parsley, onion, and celery, add the other spices, wine, and 1 cup water, and pour over the fish. Sprinkle with bread crumbs and put the slices of lemon on top. Put the fish in a 375° F. oven till tender—about ½ hour. Fry the 4 tablespoons butter with the flour, add the liquid from the fish, and make a cream sauce. Simmer for 10 minutes. Add the capers, take the sauce from the fire, and stir in the beaten egg yolks. Serve this sauce with the fish.

PIKE IN CREAM SAUCE WITH CHEESE
Snoek "au gratin"

1	pike of about 3 pounds
1	cup white wine
1	teaspoon salt
½	cup and 4 tablespoons butter
1	medium-sized onion, chopped
5	tablespoons flour
1½	cups cream
¼	teaspoon pepper
5	tablespoons grated Parmesan cheese
2	egg yolks, beaten

Bread crumbs

8 SERVINGS

Simmer the cleaned pike (see rule for cleaning under Pike) in the wine, 1 cup water, salt, and ½ cup butter till tender. Remove skin and all the bones. The meat should be in fairly large pieces. Fry the onion in the rest of the butter till golden brown. Add the flour and make a cream sauce with the cream, and about 1½ cups of the liquid from the fish, and the pepper. Simmer for 10 minutes. Stir in 3 tablespoons cheese, the egg yolks, and the fish. Pour into an ovenproof dish and sprinkle with the rest of the cheese and the bread crumbs. Let brown in moderate oven (375° F.) for ½ hour.

PIKE BALLS
Snoek balletjes

- 3 cups ground pike
- 2 thick slices white bread without crust, softened in a little milk
- ¾ teaspoon salt
- 2 eggs
- ¼ teaspoon pepper
- ½ cup ground smoked, fat fish (such as smoked eel)

8 SERVINGS

Mix all the ingredients well and form 1-inch balls. Drop them in 5 cups boiling water with salt. After 10 minutes they will be done. Drain. Served with boiled potatoes sprinkled with chopped parsley and melted butter, these balls taste exceptionally good.

STOCKFISH
Dried codfish

This is a very popular dish in the winter months, when other fish is rather scarce. It is sold dry or already softened in water by the fishmonger. First I'll give you the recipe showing how to cook it and then I'll tell you the way it is eaten in Holland.

STOCKFISH
Stokvis

1 pound dried codfish

Soften the fish overnight in plenty of water. Clean them next day and cut in long strips. Roll these up and fasten with a piece of string. Bring sufficient water to a boil—the fish must be covered. Immerse the fish in the water and reduce the heat. The fish must not boil, but simmer for about 1 hour. The time depends very much on the quality of the fish. Test it with a fork—the fish must not get soft. Drain and take the strings off.

Now we can start eating. Everybody gets a soup plate and takes a piece of fish.

> *Add to this for each person:*
> a) 2–3 boiled potatoes
> b) 2–3 spoonfuls boiled rice
> c) 2 spoonfuls fried onions
> d) Liberal amount of butter sauce
> e) The same amount of a sharp mustard sauce, and—but this is for the very brave—
> f) top with a fried egg

Mix everything on your plate and eat with a fork and spoon. It tastes excellent.

PAN FISH
Pan vis

As one always makes the dishes that go with the stock-fish, such as rice, onions, sauce, etc., in rather large quantities, there are a fair amount of leftovers the next day. Of these we prepare Pan Fish. Fry some extra onions, mix all the leftovers together, heat them topped with a liberal amount of butter, in a ovenproof dish in the oven. Served with a salad made of lettuce, cucumber, or tomato, this makes a whole meal.

Meat, poultry, and game

MEAT, POULTRY, AND GAME

The meat in America is superb, but is cut by the butcher in quite a different way from that in Holland. Nevertheless, since it plays such an important role on our daily menu in both countries, I thought that it might be a good idea to give you some of our recipes, based on similar ways of cutting the meat.

67

FILLET OR TENDERLOIN OF BEEF
Ossenhaas

1 fillet of beef of about 2 pounds
3 ounces lard
6 tablespoons butter
Salt and pepper

6 SERVINGS

Remove the surplus fat and skin and pound the fillet with the back of a knife, against the grain. Lard the meat with narrow strips. Pour a kettle of boiling water over the meat. Melt the butter in a roasting pan in the oven and brown slightly. Bake the fillet in the butter, basting all the time. (Oven temperature, 350° F.) It takes about 20 minutes to the pound, but never longer than 80 minutes. Salt and pepper are added afterward, as salt toughens the meat.

FILLET OF BEEF WITH VEGETABLES (warm)
Ossenhaas à la Jardinière

1 fillet of beef of about 2 pounds
6 tablespoons butter
Various vegetables: cauliflower, asparagus, peas,
    small carrots, champignons, Brussels sprouts,
    small tomatoes stuffed with spinach, etc.

2 tablespoons butter
2 tablespoons flour
¾ cup bouillon
¼ cup Madeira
¼ teaspoon salt

6 SERVINGS

This is a very nice dish for a dinner party. Prepare the fillet as in the previous recipe. Cut the fillet in thin slices and arrange them in the middle of the dish. Prepare all the vegetables separately and arrange them around the meat in piles, making a pleasant color combination. Fry the butter with the flour and make a smooth sauce with the bouillon. Add the meat gravy and simmer for 5 minutes. Just before serving, add the Madeira and salt. Garnish the meat with a few tablespoons of the gravy and serve the rest separately. Mashed potatoes—stir in some grated cheese—go very well with this dish.

FILLET OF BEEF WITH VEGETABLES (cold)

Prepare the fillet of beef as in Fillet of Beef with Vegetables (warm). Prepare the vegetables. Let everything cool first, then slice the meat. Marinate some of the vegetables, such as asparagus, cauliflower, and champignons. Decorate with chopped parsley and serve with mayonnaise sauce and potato salad.

MARINATED BONELESS CHUCK ROAST
Stoofvlees

1 piece of boneless chuck roast of
    about 4 pounds
1 bottle red wine
3 onions, sliced
1 bay leaf
6 cloves
1 carrot, sliced
6 peppercorns
1 teaspoon salt
1 cup butter
2 tablespoons flour
Worcestershire sauce

12 SERVINGS

Two days before you intend to eat this dish, let the meat soak in a marinade of the wine with the herbs, only partly covering the meat. Turn two or three times a day. Dry the meat. Melt the butter in a casserole, put in the meat, and turn constantly until it is a golden brown. Sprinkle with the flour and add half of the marinade. Simmer slowly with the lid on, for 1 hour, stir, and turn often. Now take the cover partly off, so that the liquid can evaporate and the sauce thickens. Simmer for 1½ hours more, adding marinade if necessary. Slice the meat and strain the sauce, adding some Worcestershire sauce or more salt.

HÂCHÉ (stewed meat)
Hâché

4 medium-sized onions, chopped
4 tablespoons fat
2 pounds round steak, cut into 1-inch cubes
3 tablespoons flour
2 tablespoons vinegar
2 bay leaves
5 cloves
1 teaspoon salt
1 tablespoon Worcestershire sauce

6 SERVINGS

Brown the onions in the fat in a heavy pan. Remove the browned onions from the pan and sauté the meat in the same fat. Add the onions, and sprinkle with the flour. Add 2 cups water and all the other ingredients. Cover the pan and simmer for about 2 hours, stirring from time to time.

This dish is eaten with boiled potatoes and red cabbage.

BEEFSTEAK
Biefstuk

1 pound beefsteak, 2 inches thick
½ cup butter
¼ teaspoon salt
Grated pepper
Milk or water

4 SERVINGS

Rub the steak with some butter. Heat the frying pan over a good flame until it is very hot. Sear the steak

quickly, first on one side, then on the other side. Reduce
the flame, add the rest of the butter, season with salt and
pepper, and broil each side for 5 minutes more. Put the
steak on a hot plate, reheat the gravy, and pour a little
milk or water in the middle of the frying pan. As soon
as the foam on the surface has disappeared, the gravy is
done. Pour over the meat.

You will find this dish on all the menus of the restaurants in Holland.

Serve with fried potatoes, a vegetable dish, and a green
salad.

BEEFSTEAK TARTARE (Cold)
Tartare biefstuk

1   pound ground round steak
1   egg yolk
1   tablespoon oil
1   teaspoon salt
1   teaspoon Worcestershire sauce
¼   teaspoon pepper
¼   teaspoon paprika
1   tablespoon chopped pickled gherkins
1   tablespoon finely chopped onions
    (optional)
1   tablespoon capers
1   teaspoon mustard

4 SERVINGS

Mix all the ingredients thoroughly. It is impossible to
give the exact amount of pepper, etc., as this is a dish
made according to one's own taste. Some people like to

add lemon juice or a little vinegar, catchup, and chopped parsley.

Serve with hot toast and butter.

BEEFSTEAK TARTARE, FRIED
Hamburger

1 pound ground round steak
1 egg yolk
1 teaspoon salt
¼ teaspoon pepper
Paprika
1 tablespoon finely chopped onions (optional)
Bread crumbs
Fat for frying
4 eggs

4 SERVINGS

Mix the meat with the egg yolk, salt, pepper, paprika, and onions. Shape into balls. Roll them in bread crumbs and fry quickly in very hot fat. The outside should be brown, but the inside raw. Top each meat ball with a fried egg. Serve with mustard.

FRESH BEEF TONGUE—BOILED
Gekookte ossetong

1 beef tongue
1 onion
1 large carrot
Sprigs of parsley and celery
½ tablespoon salt

Cover the tongue with warm water and add the other ingredients. Bring to the boil and simmer for about 3 hours. Remove the skin while still warm, starting at the point and pulling down. Put the tongue back in the liquid until you are ready to serve it, because it soon dries out. The liquid makes a very good stock for soup.

The tongue is eaten with Sour Sauce (see below) and white beans.

SOUR SAUCE
Zure saus

8 tablespoons butter
6 tablespoons flour
2 cups stock from the tongue
Juice of 1 lemon
1 egg yolk, beaten

Melt 6 tablespoons of the butter and blend in the flour. Add the stock and make a smooth sauce. Add the lemon juice and fold in the beaten egg yolk. Add the rest of the butter in small lumps, and stir until melted.

SMOKED BEEF TONGUE, BOILED
Gekookte, gerookte tong

1 smoked beef tongue
1 onion
2 bay leaves
Sprigs of parsley and celery

Soak the tongue overnight in cold water. Cover with fresh water and add the other ingredients. Bring to the boil and simmer for about 3 hours. Remove the skin (see Fresh Beef Tongue, boiled).

The tongue is eaten with Raisin Sauce.

RAISIN SAUCE
Rozijnen saus

½ cup brown sugar
1 cup stock from the tongue
½ cup raisins
Juice of ½ lemon
½ cup white wine
1 teaspoon grated lemon rind
2 tablespoons butter

Dissolve the brown sugar in the stock. Add the raisins and the lemon juice and simmer for 10 minutes. Add wine and lemon rind and stir in the butter. Slice the tongue, and serve the sauce separately.

VEAL

STUFFED BREAST OF VEAL
Gevulde kalfsborst

1 pound ground veal
3 slices white bread, soaked in milk
2 eggs
1 teaspoon salt
¼ teaspoon grated nutmeg
1 breast of veal of about 4 pounds
½ pound butter
Small can champignons (optional)

Make a stuffing of the ground veal with the bread, eggs, salt, and nutmeg. Make a cut in the breast and loosen the skin carefully. Fill with the stuffing. Brown the butter in a roasting pan and bake the meat in a slow oven (300° F.) about ½ hour to the pound. Baste every 10 minutes, adding a little cold water when the butter gets too dark, but not more than 1 cup in all. A small can of champignons may be added to the stuffing. *For the gravy:* Brown 2 tablespoons flour in 2 tablespoons butter. Add 1 cup hot stock or hot water with the drippings in which the meat has been baked. Season the gravy with salt, pepper, powdered herbs to taste (orégano, tarragon, etc.), and simmer for 10 minutes. Strain the gravy and add 1 tablespoon Madeira or sherry.

BREAST OF VEAL, STEWED
Gestoofde kalfsborst

1 breast of veal
12 tablespoons butter
8 cups bouillon
4 carrots
Sprigs of parsley and celery
Piece of mace
1 teaspoon salt
½ lemon, cut in thin slices
5 tablespoons flour
Juice of ½ lemon
1 small can champignons

6 SERVINGS

Pound the meat with the back of a knife until tender, place in colander, and pour boiling water over it. Bake in 8 tablespoons butter for 15 minutes in a moderate oven. Add the hot bouillon, carrots, parsley, celery, mace, salt, and the lemon slices. Simmer for 1¼ hours, covered.

Melt 4 tablespoons butter, blend in the flour, and make a smooth sauce with 2½ cups of the meat stock. Cook for 10 minutes; strain. Add the lemon juice and the champignons. Instead of breast, one can use other parts of veal, cut in 2-inch squares.

This dish is served with rice.

VEAL CUTLETS
Kalfscoteletten

6 veal cutlets, each ½ inch thick
Salt
Grated nutmeg (optional)
2 eggs
Bread crumbs
5 tablespoons butter

6 SERVINGS

Pour hot water over the cutlets, dry them, and sprinkle with salt and nutmeg. Drip them in the eggs diluted with 2 tablespoons water. Cover them with bread crumbs on both sides. Brown the cutlets in the butter over a low flame until they are tender, about 20 minutes, turning them six times.

FILLET STEAKS OF VEAL
Kalfsoesters

6 slices of veal cut from the round
Parsley
Lemon slices
Anchovies

6 SERVINGS

These are prepared like Veal Cutlets. When they are done, sprinkle each one with chopped parsley and top with a slice of lemon and a rolled anchovy.

STUFFED FILLETS OF VEAL
Blinde vinken

6   slices of veal cut from the round
¼   pound ground veal
1   egg
1   slice white bread, soaked in milk
Pinch salt, pepper, and nutmeg
4   tablespoons butter
2   lemon slices

6 SERVINGS

Pound the slices of veal until very thin. Mix the ground veal with the egg, bread, salt, pepper, and nutmeg. Divide into six pieces, and place each on a slice of veal. Roll the slices and tie with thread. Brown quickly in butter on all sides, add 1 tablespoon water and the lemon slices, cover, and simmer until tender, about ¾ hour.

Do not forget to take the thread off. Instead of meat stuffing, one can roll the slices around a boiled egg or use a filling of fried onions and chopped parsley.

VEAL KIDNEYS, SAUTÉED
Gebakken kalfsnieren

2   veal kidneys
2   cups bouillon
½   bay leaf
¼   teaspoon salt
¼   teaspoon pepper
½   small onion
1   egg
Bread crumbs
3   tablespoons butter

4 SERVINGS

Soak the kidneys in water for 2 hours, changing the water twice. Simmer for ½ hour in the bouillon with the bay leaf, salt, pepper, and onion. Cut them into slices. Sprinkle with salt and pepper. Dip them in the egg diluted with 2 tablespoons water, roll in the bread crumbs, and sauté them in butter.

RAGOUT OF VEAL KIDNEYS ON BREAD
Nierbroodjes

2   veal kidneys
½   bay leaf
¼   teaspoon salt
½   small onion
½   cup butter
3   tablespoons flour
½   cup cream
1   tablespoon soy sauce
1   tablespoon chopped parsley
Bread crumbs
12 slices stale white bread without crusts

12 SERVINGS

Soak the kidneys in water for 2 hours, changing the water twice. Bring fresh water to a boil with the bay leaf, salt, and onion. Add the kidneys and boil for ½ hour.

Melt 3 tablespoons butter and blend in the flour. Add 1 cup liquid (½ cream, ½ stock), soy sauce, and parsley. Cook and stir until the sauce is smooth and thick. Chop the kidneys and add to the sauce. Fry the slices of bread in butter. Divide the kidney ragout in twelve parts. Put one part on each slice of bread, sprinkle with bread crumbs (rather a thick layer), dot with butter, and put for 10 minutes in a moderate oven (325° F.).

SWEETBREADS
Zwezerik

There are many ways to prepare sweetbreads—broiled, braised, etc.—but this old recipe may be of interest to you.

SWEETBREAD PUDDING
Zwezerik pudding

2 sweetbreads
Sprigs of parsley and celery
Piece of mace
½ teaspoon salt
2 slices stale white bread, without crusts, soaked in a little cream
3 egg yolks
2 tablespoons butter, creamed
Pinch of salt and pepper
1 tablespoon chopped parsley
3 egg whites, whipped stiff

4 SERVINGS

Put the sweetbreads in a pan with water. Warm, but do not bring to a boil. Repeat this three times, using fresh water every time. Rinse them in cold water; remove the fat and membrane. Bring water to the boiling point with the parsley and celery, the piece of mace, and the salt. Simmer for 20 minutes. Drain and rinse. Reserve the stock. Remove the skin and cut the sweetbreads into small pieces. Mix these with the bread and the egg yolks;

add the butter, salt, pepper, and chopped parsley. Fold in the beaten egg whites. Pour the pudding into a greased baking dish, put in a pan with hot water, and steam in a moderate oven (350° F.) for ½ hour. Serve with Sweetbread White Sauce.

SWEETBREAD WHITE SAUCE
Witte saus

Stock from the sweetbreads
4 tablespoons butter
4 tablespoons flour
1 tablespoon brandy

Boil the sweetbread stock until reduced to 2 cups. Melt butter, add flour, and stir in the stock until the sauce is smooth and boiling. Add brandy.

PÂTÉ OF CALF'S LIVER (a cold dish)
Pâté van Kalfslever

2 pounds calf's liver
½ pound fresh fat bacon
1 small can truffles
2 tablespoons Madeira
½ pound butter
1 teaspoon salt
½ teaspoon pepper
½ teaspoon marjoram or orégano
½ teaspoon ground cloves
10 slices smoked fat bacon

8 SERVINGS

Remove the skin and veins from the calf's liver and wash in cold water. Put the liver, with ½ pound fresh bacon, through a meat chopper twice. Soak the truffles in the Madeira. Melt the butter and add all the spices, the sliced truffles, and the Madeira to the liver mixture. Mix well. Cover the bottom and sides of a pudding mold with slices of bacon, put the mixture in, and cover with the rest of the slices of bacon. Cover the pudding mold well and put in a pan of hot water. Steam in a moderate oven (350° F.) for 3 hours.

JELLIED VEAL
Kalfsvlees in gelei

2 calf's feet
1 teaspoon salt
½ bay leaf
5 ounces smoked tongue
1 small can truffles
4 dill pickles
1 envelope unflavored gelatine
¼ cup vinegar

4–6 SERVINGS

Cover the calf's feet with water, add the salt and bay leaf. Bring to a boil and simmer for 3 hours. Take the meat off the bones and put through the meat grinder. Shred the smoked tongue. Slice the truffles and dill pickles. Soften the envelope of unflavored gelatine in ½ cup cold water. Dissolve in 1 cup hot stock of the calf's feet. Add the vinegar and all the other ingredients. Mix well. Pour into moist mold, chill, and unmold.

Decorate with lettuce leaves, sliced tomato, and mayonnaise.

This is a very nice dish for a cold supper.

PORK

ROLLED RIB
Varkensschijf

4 pounds rolled rib
½ cup butter or fat
1 apple, sliced
1½ teaspoons salt
1 teaspoon marjoram or orégano
½ teaspoon pepper

8 SERVINGS

Pour a kettle of boiling water over the meat. Brown the butter or fat in a pan in the oven, add the meat, and bake in a 350° F. oven for 2 hours. After 1 hour add the sliced apple and the spices. If the roast gets too brown, add a little water to the gravy. Allow about ½ hour to the pound. Baste often.

Serve warm with cabbage or Brussels sprouts or, when cold, with fried potatoes and a green salad.

PORK CHOPS WITH PURÉE OF POTATOES AND ROBERT SAUCE
Varkenscarbonaden met purée en Robert saus

6 pork chops
Salt and pepper
4 tablespoons butter

6 SERVINGS

Sprinkle the chops with salt and pepper and spread them with butter. Heat a frying pan and sear the chops, reduce the heat, and add the rest of the butter. Cook them slowly until they are done, about 20 minutes. Heap Purée of Potatoes (see Potatoes chapter) in the middle of a dish and surround with the pork chops.

ROBERT SAUCE
Robert saus

1 tablespoon chopped onion
¼ teaspoon ground red pepper
1 bay leaf
4 cloves
2 teaspoons sugar
1 teaspoon mustard
Drippings of the pork chops and enough water to make 2 cups
4 tablespoons butter
4 tablespoons flour
1 tablespoon Madeira

Add the spices to the liquid and simmer for 20 minutes. Melt the butter, add the flour, and stir in the strained liquid, making a smooth sauce. Add the Madeira before serving.

HAM IN GELATINE
Ham-pudding

1   envelope unflavored gelatine
1½   cups bouillon
1   pound boiled ham, chopped
4   dill pickles, chopped
½   teaspoon salt
½   teaspoon pepper
2   hard-boiled eggs, chopped
Mayonnaise

Sprinkle the gelatine in cold water to soften and add to 1 cup hot stock. Stir in all the other ingredients. Put the mixture into a moist pudding mold, chill, and unmold. Serve with mayonnaise.

HAM BALLS
Hamballetjes

1 pound boiled ham, chopped
1 pound boiled potatoes, mashed
1 slice stale white bread without
   crust, softened in a little milk
3 eggs
1 teaspoon salt
1 teaspoon Worcestershire sauce
Bread crumbs
4 tablespoons butter or fat

12 BALLS

Mix all ingredients together and shape into balls. Roll them through the bread crumbs and sauté in butter.
Serve with a tomato or mustard sauce.

HAM TIMBALE
Timbale van ham

1 pound boiled ham, chopped
3 egg yolks
1 slice stale white bread without crust, soaked in a little milk
1 tablespoon chopped onion
½ cup bouillon
½ tablespoon chopped parsley
½ teaspoon salt
¼ teaspoon pepper
½ tablespoon Madeira
3 egg whites

Mix all the ingredients together except the egg whites. Beat these until stiff and fold into the mixture. Place this mixture in a greased pudding mold. Cover well and steam in a pan of hot water in a 350° F. oven for 1¼ hours and unmold.

LAMB

In Holland lamb is not a very popular dish, as it is in America and England. There are many people who have never eaten it at all, and as there is little demand, the supply is limited and the price is rather high. Therefore recipes for lamb are more suited for a dinner party. They take a little extra time to prepare, but the results make up for that.

ROAST CUSHION SHOULDER OF LAMB
Gevulde lamsborst

For the stuffing:

       2 tablespoons butter
       2 tablespoons flour
       1 onion, chopped
       1 teaspoon curry powder
       ½ apple, diced
       ½ tablespoon chopped parsley
       ½ cup water
       ½ cup milk
       ¾ cup boiled rice

For roasting:

       1 shoulder of lamb
       1 clove garlic
       1 cup butter

   6–8 SERVINGS

Make about 1 cup Curry Sauce (see Eggs in Curry Sauce in Luncheon Dishes chapter). Mix with the boiled rice. Rub the meat with a clove of garlic; one side of the meat must be open for inserting the stuffing. Stuff with the mixture of rice and Curry Sauce and secure with toothpicks. Roast the meat in the butter in a slow oven (300° F.), about 40 minutes to the pound. Baste often.

Serve with boiled rice, fried bananas, and a green salad.

LAMB CHOPS
Lamscoteletten

4 onions, chopped
4 tablespoons butter
8 lamb chops
2 tablespoons flour
1 cup bouillon
1 tablespoon vinegar
4 tomatoes, sliced
1 tablespoon chopped parsley
1 teaspoon celery salt
1 bay leaf
½ teaspoon salt
½ teaspoon paprika
2 teaspoons red currant jelly

8 SERVINGS

Sauté the onions in the butter and take them out of the skillet. Sauté the chops until they are half done; take them out too. Add the flour and make a smooth sauce, stirring in the bouillon. Place the chops in an ovenproof dish and pour the vinegar over them. Cover with the sliced tomatoes, parsley, celery salt, onions, and the sauce. Add bay leaf, salt, and paprika. Cook in a covered dish in a slow oven (300° F.) for about 3 hours. Just before serving, add the red currant jelly and some more salt if necessary.

Serve this dish with mashed potatoes and white beans.

LAMB TONGUES IN MADEIRA SAUCE
Lamstongetjes in Madeira saus

6   lamb tongues (1 per person)
1   bay leaf
Small piece of mace
Sprigs of parsley and celery
1   teaspoon salt
4   tablespoons butter
½   clove garlic, minced
4   tablespoons flour
2   tablespoons Madeira

6 SERVINGS

Cover the tongues with water. Add the spices and salt. Bring to a boil and simmer for ½ hour. Take the tongues out of the stock and trim the necks if necessary. Drain and cut into slices. Sauté these in the butter with the garlic. Add the flour and stir in 2 cups of the stock to make a smooth sauce. Add the Madeira. Sieve the sauce over the tongue.

Serve with boiled rice.

POULTRY AND GAME

In contrast with the fact that there is little taste for lamb in Holland, game and poultry are very popular here. There is still game in abundance, and great favorites of the cheaper kinds are rabbit (from the dunes) and hare (from the meadows). Since the shooting season is limited strictly by the government, the game stock is not deteriorating. Turkey is eaten a little more often at Christmas nowadays, although the traditional dish is goose.

Chicken too is still considered a Sunday treat, in spite of the fact that although it costs the same as meat, it takes a good deal more butter to prepare the necessary amount of gravy to go with the so-beloved potatoes.

ROAST CHICKEN
Gebraden kip

2   young chickens of about 2 pounds each
½ cup butter
Salt

4 SERVINGS

Chickens are often fried in a skillet on top of the stove, as many people do not have ovens. Before preparing, cut the necks and the underparts of the legs off. With the giblets, a pinch of salt, and a piece of mace, these make a delicious bouillon.

Pour boiling water over the insides and the outsides of the chickens. Season the insides of the chickens with a little salt and put a small lump of butter inside. Melt the rest of the butter in a skillet. Place the chickens in the butter and brown them for 5 minutes over a high fire, turning them often, so that they become a delicate brown on all sides. Reduce the fire, half cover the skillet with the lid, and go on roasting until the chicken is done. For a young chicken it takes 20 minutes. A fork should go in easily between the joints. Add the livers the last 5 minutes.

This dish is served with potatoes, boiled or sautéed, young green peas, and a compote.

FRIED YOUNG COCKERELS
(*in Austria: Wiener Backhähndl*)
Gebakken haantjes

4 young cockerels or young chickens
Pinch of salt
Flour
2 eggs
Bread crumbs
Oil

4 SERVINGS

Leave the chickens for 2 minutes in boiling water. Rinse with cold water. Cut open lengthwise and take out the largest bones. Now cut crosswise once. Sprinkle with salt and dredge them lightly with flour. Beat the eggs with 4 tablespoons water. Roll the pieces through the egg mixture, then through the bread crumbs. They should be well covered on all sides. Heat the oil and fry the pieces.

CHICKEN IN TOMATO SAUCE
Kip met tomaten saus

2 chickens of about 2 pounds each
½ cup butter
1¼ cups bouillon
2 tablespoons flour
4 tablespoons tomato purée
1 tablespoon chopped celery, stalks
   and leaves
1 teaspoon grated onion
1 teaspoon sugar
½ teaspoon salt
¼ teaspoon pepper

4 SERVINGS

Pour boiling water over the chickens, outside and inside. Sauté the chickens in butter until they are brown on all sides. Cut each in four pieces. Put them back in the pan and add the bouillon and the other ingredients. Cover and bake in a slow oven (325° F.) for about ¾ hour. Place the pieces of chicken on a dish and strain the sauce.

Serve this dish with macaroni or spaghetti and grated cheese.

GALANTINE OF CHICKEN
(*Pressed chicken*)
Galantine van kip

1	stewing chicken of about 5 pounds

For the stuffing:

¾	pound veal
3	ounces lard
1	3-ounce slice smoked ox tongue
1	small can truffles
1	slice stale white bread without crust, soaked in a little milk
4	egg yolks
1	teaspoon salt
2	dill pickles, sliced
2	tablespoons Madeira

Salt and pepper

For cooking:

5	thin slices fat bacon
6	cups bouillon
3	carrots

Sprigs of parsley and celery

Put the veal and the lard through the meat chopper. Dice the tongue and the truffles. Mix all the ingredients for the stuffing very well. Pour boiling water over the chicken. Cut the breast open and disjoint it. Sprinkle a little salt and pepper in the chicken and put the stuffing inside. Close the breast by sewing it together.

Fasten the slices of bacon onto the breast with thread. Roll the chicken in a piece of cheesecloth. Put in a pan with the bouillon, carrots, parsley, celery, and salt. The chicken should be covered; otherwise, add some water. Bring to a boil and simmer for 2 hours. Let cool in the stock.

Place the chicken between two boards with a weight on top—a vase filled with water will do—and let stand for 3 hours. Remove the cheesecloth and take off the thread and bacon.

Decorate this dish with quartered tomatoes, eggs, lettuce leaves, etc. Serve with a light Mayonnaise (see Sauces chapter).

ASPIC (for decoration)
Aspic

2 envelopes unflavored gelatine
2 cups stock, strained
2 bouillon cubes
2 tablespoons vinegar
1 tablespoon sherry

Soften the gelatine in ½ cup water. Bring the stock to a boil. Add the bouillon cubes, vinegar, and sherry. Stir in the gelatine and water until dissolved. Pour into a shallow dish and chill thoroughly. Cut into different shapes and break up what is left with a fork.

PARTRIDGES WITH CABBAGE
Patrijzen met kool

4　partridges
Salt
12　slices fat bacon
½　cup butter
1　big or 2 small heads cabbage
2　onions, chopped
1　teaspoon pepper
¼　teaspoon grated nutmeg

6 SERVINGS

Pour boiling water over the birds and rub them with salt. Place the slices of bacon, 3 to each bird, over the breasts and tie with thread. Melt the butter in a baking dish and roast the partridges like chickens in a moderate oven (350° F.) for 40 minutes, basting often.

Shred the cabbage, cook for 10 minutes, and drain well. Put half of it in a casserole. Remove the bacon from the partridges and cut the birds lengthwise in halves. Place them on the cabbage in the casserole and cover with the rest of the cabbage.

Sauté the chopped onions in the same skillet and add water to make 2 cups of stock. Chop the bacon that has covered the breasts and add this to the stock. Sprinkle the cabbage with pepper and nutmeg. Pour in the stock. Cover the casserole and put in a 350° F. oven for 2 hours.

Serve with boiled potatoes.

PÂTÉ OF PARTRIDGES
Patrijzen pâté

This is an old recipe, but very useful, as old partridges can be used. Turkey could be used too, although I have never tried that out myself. It is a very nice dish for a cold supper.

4 old partridges
1¼ cups butter
½ pound uncooked veal
4 tablespoons flour
6 egg yolks
3 ounces grated Parmesan cheese
1 teaspoon salt
½ teaspoon pepper

Roast the birds (as in the recipe for Roast Chicken) in ½ cup butter. Remove skin and bones and put them, with the veal, through a meat chopper twice. Melt 4 tablespoons butter, add the flour, stir in 2 cups of bouillon made with partridge gravy diluted with water, and make a smooth sauce. Whip ½ cup butter until creamy. Stir into the sauce one by one the egg yolks, cheese, meat, creamy butter, salt, and pepper. Mix well.

Press this mixture into a well-greased baking tin, the kind that is used to bake cakes in. Put the tin in a pan with boiling water and bake in a moderate oven (325° F.) for 2 hours. Cool and unmold the next day. Cut into slices and decorate with Aspic (see recipe for Aspic).

ROAST GOOSE
Gebraden gans

1 goose
10 sour apples, sliced
½ cup butter
Salt and pepper

8 SERVINGS

Pour boiling water over the inside and outside of the goose. Fill the body cavity with the sliced apples and secure with skewers, or sew it up. Melt the butter in a roasting pan and roast the goose in a moderate oven (325° F.), allowing 25 minutes to the pound. Baste every 15 minutes. When the goose is half done, sprinkle with salt and pepper. Should the breast get too brown, cover with a piece of greased wax paper or aluminum foil.

ROAST PHEASANT
Gebraden fazant

1 pheasant
6 tablespoons butter
Salt

3 SERVINGS

Pour boiling water over the pheasant, inside and outside. Sprinkle a little salt inside the bird and put in a lump of butter. Take a skillet as small as possible; the bird should just fit in it. Brown the butter, place the pheasant for a short time on the breast side, then turn it over. Cover and roast in 350° F. oven for ½ hour. Baste three or four times.

Serve the pheasant with the following sauce.

SAUCE FOR ROAST PHEASANT

2½ tablespoons flour
1½ cups heavy cream
½ teaspoon salt
2 tablespoons brandy
½ tablespoon Worcestershire sauce

Pour off all but 3 tablespoons of the drippings. Add the flour and let this get slightly brown. Stir well. Add the heavy cream and the salt. Cook and stir until sauce is creamy and smooth. Stir in the brandy and the Worcestershire sauce.

ROAST DUCK
Gebraden eend

1 wild duck
Salt and pepper
6 tablespoons butter
1 sour apple

2 SERVINGS

Pour boiling water over the duck, inside and outside. Rub the inside with salt and pepper and put in the apple. Take the smallest possible pan. Melt the butter and put in the duck with the apple inside. Cover and roast in a moderate over (325° F.) for 1½ hours, basting every 10 minutes. The duck is done when a fork goes in easily between the joints.

STUFFED DUCK
Gevulde eend

1 cup chestnuts
1 duck
6 tablespoons butter
Salt and pepper

2 SERVINGS

Make two cross-cut gashes over the flat side of each chestnut. Boil them for 5 minutes in water, drain, and peel. Cover them with water or stock and cook for 20 minutes. Prepare the duck as in recipe for Roast Duck. Put the chestnuts inside and roast the duck.

SALMI OF DUCKS
Salmi van eend

2   ducks
½   cup butter
4   cups stock
4   carrots
3   small onions
½   bay leaf
½   teaspoon salt
4   tablespoons flour
1   small can champignons
2   tablespoons Madeira

4 SERVINGS

Sauté the ducks in 6 tablespoons butter. Add stock, carrots, 2 onions, bay leaf, and salt. Bring to a boil and simmer for 2 hours. Take the duck out of the stock and cut the meat off the bones in equal pieces. Put the bones back in the stock, bring to a boil, and reduce stock to 2 cups. Chop the remaining onion and sauté in 2 tablespoons butter. Add flour and brown. Strain the stock and add to this mixture. Stir well, making a smooth sauce. Put the duck back into the sauce. Add champignons and simmer for 15 minutes. Add Madeira just before serving.

HARE OR RABBIT
Haas of konijn

Do not forget that hares and rabbits are a favorite dish in Holland and therefore there are many recipes to choose from. One does not see them on the menu in the United States very often, but I hope that these recipes may serve to make this dish more popular.

ROAST HARE
Gebraden haas

1   hare
1   bottle vinegar
Salt
Mustard
4   slices of fat, smoked bacon,
     ¼ inch thick, cut into strips
½ pound butter
1   cup sour cream
½ cup blood
½ cup red wine

6 SERVINGS

Marinate the hare in the vinegar for a couple of hours. Take it out and pour boiling water over it. Sprinkle with salt and rub with mustard. Lard (with a larding pin) the back of the hare by drawing one row of thin strips of fat, smoked bacon through it—2 rows through the hind legs. Melt the butter, but do not let it get brown, and roast the hare for 2–2½ hours in a 350° F. oven, basting every 10 minutes. If the butter gets too brown, baste with sour cream. The hare is done when the meat from the hind legs can be taken off with a spoon. An old hare takes more time, of course. In that case one covers the hare with a greased piece of wax paper or aluminum foil, because otherwise the back would get too dry. Take the hare out of the pan. Mix the blood with the wine and stir into the sauce, but do not heat the sauce again.

Serve with boiled potatoes, red cabbage and apple-sauce.

STEWED HARE OR RABBIT
Gestoofde haas of konijn

1   hare or 2 rabbits
½ pound and 2 tablespoons butter
Salt and pepper
6   slices fat, smoked bacon
2   cups sour cream
4   tablespoons flour
1   cup bouillon
1   teaspoon grated lemon rind

6 SERVINGS

Cut the legs in two, the rump in six, pieces. Sauté in butter for 20 minutes. Sprinkle with salt and pepper. Cover the bottom of a pot with bacon slices and cover these with the rabbit pieces and the drippings. Pour in the sour cream. Cover the pot well and steam in a 325° F. oven for 2½–3 hours. Take the game out. Mix 2 tablespoons butter and the flour with a fork on a plate and add to the sauce. Stir in the bouillon; you should have a cream sauce—and not too thin. Pour through a fine sieve. Add some extra pepper and the grated lemon rind.

HAZEPEPER
A spicy dish of hare

1	large hare
1	cup vinegar
3	cups red wine
1	cup and 2 tablespoons butter
2	onions, sliced
5	tablespoons flour
2	teaspoons sugar
1	teaspoon salt
½	teaspoon pepper
1	bay leaf
4	cloves
2	tablespoons soy sauce

Cut a large hare into ten or twelve pieces. Marinate these overnight in vinegar and wine. Drain and sauté in ½ cup butter for 15 minutes. Sauté the onions in the rest of the butter, add flour, and brown. Stir in the wine-and-vinegar mixture and make a smooth sauce. Add hare and onions with the butter they are sautéed in, add sugar and spices, and simmer for at least 3 hours.

PÂTÉ OF HARE OR RABBIT
Hazen-of konijnenpastei

1 hare or 2 rabbits
½ pound veal
½ pound fresh bacon
4 egg yolks
1 teaspoon ground mixed spices
½ teaspoon salt
12 slices fat, smoked bacon

Stew hare or rabbits as in recipe for Stewed Hare or Rabbit. Take all the meat off the bones, keeping aside the big pieces. Put the small pieces with the veal and fresh bacon through a meat chopper twice. Add egg yolks, mixed spice, salt and ¾ cup sauce from the stew. Mix well. Cover the sides and bottom of a pudding mold with bacon slices. Put in alternate layers of the mixture and the big pieces of game. The top layer should consist of the mixture. Cover and put into a pan with boiling water. Steam in a 325° F. oven for 2 hours. Cool for ½ hour and unmold. Chill before serving.

This is a nice dish to start a dinner, served with toast and butter.

SAUCES

It is impossible to give you recipes from Holland without mentioning the best known of all sauces: the Hollandaise sauce. The only trouble with this sauce is that there are so many different ways of preparing it. The original sauce is rather difficult to make and has to be served at once, which can create great difficulties without a "Cordon Bleu" in the kitchen.

HOLLANDAISE SAUCE
Hollandaise saus

Pinch of salt
2   egg yolks
8   tablespoons butter
½   teaspoon lemon juice
1   cup cold water

Put some water in the lower half of a double boiler—
there should be a space of about ½ inch between the
bottom of the top half and the surface of the water.
Put this on the heat. Meanwhile mix together ½ tablespoon of cold water with a pinch of salt, the egg yolks,
and 1 tablespoon butter. When the water in the bottom
half is nearly, but not quite boiling, put the top half on
and start stirring with a wire whisk until the mixture
begins to thicken very slightly. Add another piece of
butter and so on until all the butter is used up. Now, the
point of the cup of cold water is this: if the sauce is
thickening too much, add ¼ teaspoonful of water from
the cup. This makes the sauce cook as slowly as possible
and makes it lighter too. Add ½ teaspoon of lemon juice,
or more, according to your taste. If you have to keep the
sauce waiting for a few minutes, do so in the double
boiler, but the water in the bottom half should not come
too near the boiling point.

If the butter starts to clarify and the eggs to curdle
during this process, immediately take the top half off the
stove, add a tablespoon of very cold water, and stir
vigorously until the sauce becomes smooth again.

MOCK HOLLANDAISE SAUCE
Namaak Hollandaise saus

    1 teaspoon arrowroot
 ± 6 tablespoons milk
    3 egg yolks
    8 tablespoons butter
    ½ teaspoon lemon juice
    Pinch of salt and pepper

4 SERVINGS

Mix the arrowroot with 3 tablespoons cold milk. Stir in the egg yolks and 1 tablespoon butter. Place the pan over a very low flame. Whisk with a wire whisk until the sauce looks like a very creamy scrambled egg. Take the pan off the heat and stir in another tablespoon butter. Keep on doing this, off and on the heat, until you have added 8 tablespoons butter in all. Toward the end, stir in some more milk; the sauce should not become too thick. Stir in the lemon juice and a pinch of salt and pepper.

MAYONNAISE

    1 egg yolk
    Pinch of salt
    1 teaspoon vinegar or lemon juice
    8 tablespoons oil

3 SERVINGS

To make a good (and quick) mayonnaise it is necessary that all ingredients have the same temperature, more or less.

Beat the egg yolk in a bowl with a pinch of salt; one gets the best results with a wire whisk. Add 1 teaspoon vinegar and stir well. The first tablespoon of oil should be added slowly, but as soon as the sauce thickens, one can put in a tablespoon at a time. Every time the sauce gets too thick, add a few drops of vinegar or lemon juice. For three persons, 8 tablespoons of oil is sufficient, but one can easily use more. With 2 egg yolks one can make mayonnaise for at least 6–8 servings.

To start with adding the vinegar is a much quicker method than to start with stirring in the oil drop by drop, and it gives the best results.

With mayonnaise as a base one can make the following sauces:

1. Add chopped herbs (parsley, celery, tarragon, etc.)
2. Add chopped dill pickles and capers
3. Add paprika
4. Add catchup and whipped cream

In addition to the above sauces, I have, throughout the book, given the recipes for other sauces. They follow directly the recipes for dishes that they may accompany.

Amsterdam vegetable market

VEGETABLES

Vegetables are an important part of the daily Dutch menu. Although all kinds can be obtained the year round, canned or frozen, vegetables are usually eaten fresh, in season.

Early every morning the vegetables are brought into town to be sold at the greengrocers' and in little stalls at the vegetable markets. These stalls make a pretty, colorful picture. The fresh, sparkling greens are mixed with the bright red of tomatoes and radishes in early spring and summer. Orange carrots brighten the darker hues of green and red cabbages in autumn and winter.

Every season is represented by its own special kinds of fruit and vegetables, and the greengrocer really is the "merchant of the four seasons," as he is called in France.

Vegetables are sometimes mixed with potatoes and meat or bacon and served as a one-pot meal.

SPINACH
Spinazie

6 pounds fresh spinach
1 tablespoon salt
6 tablespoons butter
3 slices white bread, cut into strips
3 hard-boiled eggs, quartered
Lemon quarters

6 SERVINGS

Clean the spinach thoroughly and cook with the salt for about 15 minutes. Drain and chop very finely. Add 4 tablespoons butter and reheat. Fry the strips of bread in 2 tablespoons butter; in Dutch they are called *soldaatjes*, or little soldiers, as one puts them upright on the spinach. Put the egg quarters in between the croutons on the dish. Serve lemon quarters separately.

SORREL
Zuring

2 pounds sorrel
3 tablespoons butter
3 tablespoons sugar

4 SERVINGS

Strip and wash the sorrel; cook without water. Drain, and simmer with the butter and sugar.

To make a very old-fashioned dish, add 2 tablespoons raisins.

ASPARAGUS

Asparagus is considered a great delicacy in Holland. Late spring–early summer is the season in which one can buy them. The all-white variety or the white asparagus with purple heads are grown here, but the following recipes can just as well be used for other kinds, such as the green ones.

Asparagus can be prepared and eaten in many different ways, but let us start with the typical Dutch one.

ASPARAGUS
Asperges

± 12 asparagus
2 hard-boiled eggs
¼ teaspoon grated nutmeg
Salt

1 SERVING

Scrape the asparagus with care and cut the stalky ends off. Boil in ample water till done, minimum 1 hour. When the cooked asparagus are served, one makes the following paste on one's plate: Mash the eggs very finely with a fork in the melted Butter Sauce (see below). Sprinkle with nutmeg and salt to taste. The asparagus is taken carefully in the left hand and—with the fork in the right hand—is lightly dipped in this paste. The ends, which may be a bit stalky, are left on the side of the plate.

The butter sauce that goes with it can be made in two ways:

MELTED BUTTER SAUCE I
Gewelde boter I

3 tablespoons butter

1 SERVING

This is the easier way. Melt 2 tablespoons butter slowly, so that the yellow color does not change. Never brown it. Remove from heat and add the third tablespoon; stir well until all has melted.

MELTED BUTTER SAUCE II
Gewelde boter II

6 tablespoons butter
Salt

4 SERVINGS

Stir the butter till it becomes creamy and add 1 tablespoon warm water very slowly, stirring all the time. It should be a creamy sauce. Salt to taste.

ASPARAGUS À LA CRÊME
Asperges in roomsaus

18 asparagus stalks
1 tablespoon salt
2 tablespoons butter
2 tablespoons flour
½ cup cream

4 SERVINGS

Scrape the asparagus with care, cut into 1½-inch lengths—leave out the stalky ends—and cook in boiling water with salt until done.

Mix the butter and the flour over low heat, add cream and ½ cup asparagus liquid. Stir well; keep at boiling point for 10 minutes. Simmer the asparagus in the sauce.

ASPARAGUS AU GRATIN
Asperges au gratin

18 asparagus stalks
1 teaspoon salt
1 tablespoon flour
1½ tablespoons butter
½ cup cream
½ cup broth
½ teaspoon grated nutmeg
¼ cup minced lean ham
2 tablespoons Parmesan cheese

4 SERVINGS

Cook the asparagus as in the recipe for Asparagus à la Crême.

Place the asparagus in a baking dish, cover with the sauce, made with the flour, 1 tablespoon butter, cream, broth, and nutmeg, minced ham, grated cheese, and dot with the remaining ½ tablespoon butter. Brown in moderate oven (350° F.) for about 20 minutes.

CAULIFLOWER
Bloemkool

1 medium-sized head cauliflower
1 tablespoon salt

4 SERVINGS

Cook in ample boiling water with salt for about ½ hour. To preserve the white color, cook with stem upward. After draining thoroughly, place the cauliflower on a platter and cover with Cauliflower Sauce (see below).

CAULIFLOWER SAUCE
Bloemkool saus

2   tablespoons butter
2   tablespoons flour
½ cup hot milk
Pinch of salt
Grated nutmeg

4 SERVINGS

Melt the butter. Stir in the flour until blended. Slowly stir in the milk and ½ cup cauliflower liquid. Cook and stir until the sauce is smooth and boiling. Add salt to taste and season with grated nutmeg.

CAULIFLOWER AU GRATIN
Bloemkool au gratin

1	large head cauliflower
3½	tablespoons butter
3	tablespoons flour
3	cups milk
¼	teaspoon salt
¼	teaspoon pepper
3	tablespoons grated Gruyère cheese
3	tablespoons grated Parmesan cheese
2	tablespoons bread crumbs

6 SERVINGS

Cook the cauliflower as in the recipe for Cauliflower. Mix 2 tablespoons butter and the flour over low heat, add the milk, the salt and pepper. Keep the sauce at the boiling point for about 10 minutes. Remove from heat and stir in the 3 tablespoons Gruyère cheese. Place the cauliflower in a baking dish. Cover with the sauce and sprinkle with the 3 tablespoons Parmesan cheese. Cover with 1½ tablespoons melted butter and sprinkle with bread crumbs. Brown in moderate oven (350° F.) for 20 minutes.

RHUBARB
Rabarber

1½	pounds rhubarb stems
½	cup sugar (more if necessary)
1	teaspoon grated lemon rind
1	egg yolk
1	egg white

6 SERVINGS

Peel off the outer rind, cut the rhubarb into 1-inch pieces, and wash. Cook with ½ cup water to a mash, stirring frequently. When the mash is ready, add the sugar and the lemon rind. Stir in the yolk and the white of an egg, beaten separately.

BRAISED LETTUCE
Stoofsla

16 heads lettuce
1 tablespoon salt
1 cup meat gravy
3 tablespoons butter
2 tablespoons bread crumbs

6 SERVINGS

Remove the outer green leaves from the lettuce and wash the heads thoroughly. Cook in ample boiling water with salt for ¼ hour. Drain well and place in baking dish. Cover with the gravy, dot with butter, and sprinkle with the bread crumbs. Heat in moderate oven (350° F.) for about 15 minutes.

STUFFED LETTUCE
Gevulde stoofsla

12 heads lettuce
1 slice white bread
1 pound ground veal
¼ teaspoon grated nutmeg
1 teaspoon salt
2 cups stock
1 tablespoon butter
1 tablespoon bread crumbs

6 SERVINGS

Take off the outer leaves. Quickly boil the lettuce heads in water till tender. Drain. Soften the bread in a little water and mix with the ground veal, nutmeg, and salt. Divide the mixture into 12 little balls, open the lettuce heads, and put a ball inside each head. Arrange in a baking dish, pour in the stock (2 bouillon cubes dissolved in 2 cups of hot water will do instead of stock). Dot with butter and sprinkle with the bread crumbs. Brown in moderate oven (350° F.) for 20 minutes.

(BELGIAN) ENDIVE I
Brussels lof I

1½ pounds (8 pieces) endive
1 teaspoon salt
2 tablespoons melted butter
¼ teaspoon grated nutmeg

4 SERVINGS

Cook the endive (without cutting) in water and salt until tender, about ½ hour. Drain well. Arrange in a shallow baking dish, cover with butter, sprinkle with nutmeg, and put in a hot oven (450° F.) for 10 minutes.

(BELGIAN) ENDIVE II
Brussels lof II

1½ pounds (8 pieces) endive
1 teaspoon salt
4 tablespoons melted butter
4 hard-boiled eggs, cut in quarters

4 SERVINGS

Boil the endive (without cutting) in water and salt until tender, about ½ hour. Drain well. Melt the butter.

Garnish the endive with the hard-boiled eggs and serve the butter sauce separately.

(BELGIAN) ENDIVE III
Brussels lof III

1½ pounds endive
1   teaspoon salt
2   tablespoons **butter**
3   tablespoons **flour**
1   cup milk
2   tablespoons grated Parmesan cheese

4 SERVINGS

Cut the endive into pieces. Wash and boil in salted water until tender. Drain well. Make a sauce of the butter, flour, and milk. Stir in half of the cheese. When this is melted, add the endive. Put in baking dish and sprinkle with the rest of the cheese. Bake in a hot oven (450° F.) for 15 minutes.

BRUSSELS SPROUTS
Spruitjes

4   cups Brussels sprouts
1   teaspoon salt
3   tablespoons butter
½   teaspoon grated nutmeg

4 SERVINGS

Remove the outer leaves and cut off the stems. Wash thoroughly and cook the sprouts in ample salted water. Drain well and simmer with the butter and the nutmeg.

BRUSSELS SPROUTS WITH CHEESE
Spruitjes met kaas

4 cups Brussels sprouts
1 teaspoon salt
1 cup stock
2 tablespoons grated Parmesan cheese
½ teaspoon grated nutmeg
1 tablespoon butter

4 SERVINGS

Cook the sprouts as in the recipe for Brussels Sprouts. Drain well. Put in a shallow baking dish. Pour the stock (or 1 bouillon cube dissolved in water) over the sprouts and sprinkle with the cheese and the nutmeg. Dot with butter and bake in a hot oven (450° F.) until the cheese is melted.

PURÉE OF BRUSSELS SPROUTS
Spruiten purée

4 cups Brussels sprouts
1 teaspoon salt
1 teaspoon grated nutmeg
½ cup cream

4 SERVINGS

Cook the Brussels sprouts in the usual manner. Rub through a sieve. Add salt and nutmeg and stir in the cream. This purée goes very well with duck or pork.

WHITE CABBAGE
Witte kool

1 large head white cabbage
Salt
3 tablespoons butter
½ cup milk

6 SERVINGS

Remove outer leaves and core. Cut in pieces. Wash the cabbage thoroughly and cook in boiling water and salt for about ½ hour. Drain well. Chop very fine and simmer with the butter, milk, and 1 teaspoon salt.

WHITE CABBAGE WITH POTATOES
Stamppot witte kool

1 head white cabbage
4 cups peeled and quartered potatoes
Salt
4 ounces bacon fat or lard

4 SERVINGS

Cook the cabbage as in the recipe for White Cabbage. Cover the potatoes with 2 cups water; add salt and fat. Put the cooked cabbage on top of the potatoes as soon as they are done. Mix well.

This dish is eaten as a whole meal and is a typical "winter dish." Meat is not necessary, although frankfurters or pork chops go very well with it.

RED CABBAGE
Rode kool

1 medium-sized head red cabbage
¼ cup vinegar
4 tablespoons butter
4½ tablespoons brown sugar
1 teaspoon salt
4 sour apples, cut in quarters
1 teaspoon mixed spice

4 SERVINGS

Remove the outer leaves of the cabbage and shred it fine. Cook with all other ingredients and 1 cup water, but use only 2 tablespoons of the butter. Cook the cabbage for 1 hour, stirring now and then and adding water if necessary. Add the rest of the butter before serving.

STEWED ONIONS
Gestoofde uien

1 pound onions
½ tablespoon salt
2 tablespoons butter
2 tablespoons flour
Juice of ½ lemon
1 cup stock

2 SERVINGS

Clean and slice the onions. Cook in boiling water and salt till tender. Drain well. Make a sauce of the butter, flour, and lemon juice with the stock. Simmer the onions in this sauce for 10 minutes.

STUFFED ONIONS
Gevulde uien

4 large onions
1 slice white bread, softened in a little water
5 ounces ground beef
¼ teaspoon salt
2 tablespoons butter
1 cup stock
2 tablespoons bread crumbs

4 SERVINGS

Don't slice the onions for this recipe; cook them in boiling water till tender. Drain well.

Mix the softened bread with the meat and salt. Divide into four parts. Scoop out the onions; chop and reserve insides. Stuff onions with the meat. Arrange in a greased baking dish. Press a large dot of butter in each onion. Mix the stock with the insides of the onions and pour in the dish. Sprinkle with the bread crumbs and bake in a moderate oven (350° F.) for ½ hour.

BRAISED LEEKS
Gestoofde prei

2   pounds leeks
2½ tablespoons butter
2   tablespoons flour
1   cup milk
1   tablespoon vinegar
¼   teaspoon salt

4 SERVINGS

Clean the leeks by cutting off the roots and removing the outer leaves. Cut in 2-inch lengths. Cook in boiling water for about ½ hour. Drain well. Make a sauce of the butter, flour, and milk. Add the vinegar and salt. Simmer the leeks in the sauce for about 10 minutes.

RED BEETS
Bieten

6   Small beets
2   onions
2   tablespoons butter
2   tablespoons flour
½   cup milk
½   cup water
4   cloves
Pinch of salt
2   tablespoons vinegar

4 SERVINGS

Wash the beets and cook them in water till the skin can be pulled off easily. In the winter this takes 3 to 4 hours; in the summer, 2 to 2½ hours. In Holland they are usually sold cooked, which makes it much easier, of course. Chop the onions. Make a sauce of the butter and flour with milk and water. Peel the beets and cut them in thin slices. Add these, with the chopped onions, the cloves, and the salt, to the sauce and stew for 20 minutes. Stir in the vinegar and take the cloves out before serving.

BEET SALAD (Cold)
Bietensla

6 beets
6 boiled potatoes, cold
4 hard-boiled eggs
2 apples
3 large sour gherkins
Mayonnaise or oil and vinegar
Salt and pepper

4 SERVINGS

Cook the beets as in previous recipe. Peel and cut them in small dice. Chop all the other ingredients and mix with the beets. Mix with mayonnaise, or, if this is considered to be too nourishing, use oil and vinegar. Add salt and pepper to taste. The salad should be of a rather solid consistency.

This dish is a great favorite with cold meat.

WINTER DISHES

To end this chapter, I will give you the recipes for some typical winter dishes. They can all be prepared in advance, which makes the flavor even better. They are easy to prepare and taste very good when one has been in the open for a whole day.

NOTE 1   For these dishes one uses fat, lard, or, if these are not obtainable, fat bacon that one melts slowly.

NOTE 2   With these dishes we eat a kind of sausage called *rookworst*. It has a smoked and spicy taste and has to be cooked very slowly. Knockwurst or frankfurters would be the best equivalent.

KALE WITH POTATOES AND SAUSAGE

Stamppot van boerenkool met worst

4 pounds kale
4 pounds potatoes, peeled and quartered
1-pound can of frankfurters or
  other sausage (see NOTE 2)
5 tablespoons fat (see NOTE 1)
1 teaspoon salt

6 SERVINGS

Strip the kale, wash, and boil for about 1 hour. Drain and mince very fine. Take a big pot and first put in the potatoes, half covered with water. Put the kale on top of the potatoes with the fat and salt, and simmer. If necessary, add some of the liquid from the frankfurters. The result (after about ½ hour) must be rather dry. Mix thoroughly. Put in a dish with the hot frankfurters— or boiled knockwurst, if available—on top.

HODGEPODGE WITH BOILED MEAT
Hutspot met klapstuk

2 pounds of boiling beef (flank)
2 teaspoons salt
5 pounds carrots
3 pounds potatoes
9 big onions
Pepper

8 SERVINGS

Put the meat with the salt in 4 cups boiling water and let it cook slowly for about 1½ hours, depending on the quality of the meat.

Clean and dice the carrots and add them to the meat. Let cook ½ hour. Cut the potatoes and onions in pieces and add these to the meat and the carrots. Simmer until the liquid has nearly evaporated. Add water if necessary. When this dish is ready, take out the meat and serve separately. Stir the vegetables and potatoes with a wooden spoon till they have the consistency of a stew. Add pepper to taste.

HODGEPODGE WITH WHITE BEANS AND SALT PORK
Hutspot met witte bonen en spek

2 pounds salt pork
5 pounds carrots, diced
3 pounds potatoes, peeled and quartered
9 large onions, cut in pieces
1 large can white beans

8 SERVINGS

Boil the salt pork in 4 cups water. Taste, and if the water is too salty, add fresh water. Add the carrots, onions, and potatoes, and cook till nearly done. Take the salt pork out. Stir the vegetables and let them cook till they have the consistency of a stew. Add the beans and the salt pork, cut in thin slices. Reheat.

SAUERKRAUT WITH POTATOES, BACON, AND FRANKFURTERS
Stamppot van zuurkool met spek en worst

3   pounds sauerkraut
5   pounds potatoes, quartered
1½ pounds fresh salted bacon
1   large can frankfurters

8 SERVINGS

Rinse the sauerkraut with clear water. Put it in a big pot and add fresh water to cover. Let cook slowly for about ½ hour. Add the potatoes and the bacon and simmer for about 40 minutes. Take the bacon out and cook until the liquid has evaporated. Mix well. Serve on a plate with slices of bacon and top with heated frankfurters.

APPLES WITH POTATOES AND FRIED BACON
"Hete bliksem"

Meaning that this dish is hot as lightning. Eat carefully, otherwise you may burn your mouth!

4 pounds potatoes, peeled and quartered
2 pounds sweet apples, peeled and cut up
2 pounds sour apples, peeled and cut up
4 tablespoons lard
16 slices smoked bacon

8 SERVINGS

Half cover the potatoes with water. Start boiling. Add the apples and the lard. Boil slowly, stirring often, till the mixture has the consistency of a purée. Add water if necessary. Fry the bacon till crisp and serve on top.

BROWN BEANS
Bruine bonen

2 pounds dried brown beans
1 teaspoon salt
1 pound fat smoked bacon
6 onions, cut into rings

8 SERVINGS

Wash the brown beans and let them stand overnight in plenty of water. Cook the beans the next day in the same water for about 1 hour, making sure that there is always enough water to cover the beans. Add salt. Drain, keeping the water for soup. Dice the bacon fine. Fry it in a frying pan till very crisp. Mix through the beans. Fry the onions in the fat that is left in the frying pan. Serve these separately.

Sour dill pickles and mustard accompany this nourishing dish.

POTATOES

Potatoes are a national dish in Holland. This may sound strange to Americans, who—if they eat them at all—eat them as a side dish. But a meal eaten by the farmers and in the villages consists in the first and only place of an enormous dish of potatoes which is put in the middle of the table. All the members of the family gather around, armed with a cup and fork. In this cup is gravy, if they have recently butchered a pig and fried the meat; otherwise bacon fat is used.

Now everybody in turn (old grandfather starting) picks a potato out of the big pan in the middle with his own fork, dips it in the fat in his own cup, and eats. Two pounds per person is the usual portion, children included. No plates, no nothing—easy, what? Even van Gogh was inspired by this family scene and painted one of his most famous pictures.

But of course, since potatoes play such an important role in Dutch life, there are many other ways of preparing them.

PURÉE OF POTATOES I
Aardappel-purée I

1 pound boiled potatoes
¾ cup milk
2 tablespoons butter
½ teaspoon salt
⅛ teaspoon nutmeg
1 egg yolk, beaten
1 egg white, whipped stiff
1 tablespoon bread crumbs

3 SERVINGS

Rub the potatoes through a sieve. Blend in the milk, 1 tablespoon butter, the salt, nutmeg, and the beaten egg yolk; fold in the beaten egg white. Put the purée in a baking dish slightly greased with butter. Sprinkle with bread crumbs and dot with the remaining butter. Put in a moderate oven (350° F.) for 20 minutes.

PURÉE OF POTATOES II
Aardappel-purée II

1   pound boiled potatoes
¾   cup milk
3   tablespoons butter
½   teaspoon salt
⅛   teaspoon grated nutmeg
Pinch of pepper
1   egg

3 SERVINGS

Rub the boiled potatoes through a sieve. Heat the milk with the butter, salt, nutmeg, and pepper and add to the potatoes. Keep on a slow fire for 15 minutes, stirring all the time. Beat the whole egg and stir in just before serving.

PURÉE OF POTATOES WITH CHEESE
Aardappel-purée met kaas

2   pounds boiled potatoes
2   eggs
1   cup sour cream
½   teaspoon salt
3   tablespoons grated Parmesan cheese
2   tablespoons butter
1   tablespoon bread crumbs

6 SERVINGS

Rub the boiled potatoes through a sieve. Beat the eggs with the sour cream and the salt. Add 2 tablespoons of the cheese and mix with the purée. Grease a baking dish with some of the butter. Put the purée inside and sprinkle with 1 tablespoon cheese mixed with 1 tablespoon bread crumbs. Dot with the rest of the butter and bake for ½ hour in a moderate oven (350° F.).

PURÉE OF POTATOES WITH HAM AND ONIONS
Aardappel-purée met ham en uien

2   pounds boiled potatoes
1   cup milk
½   teaspoon salt
2   medium-sized onions chopped fine
3   tablespoons butter
¼   pound diced ham
1   tablespoon bread crumbs

6 SERVINGS

Rub the boiled potatoes through a sieve. Stir in the milk and salt. Fry the onions in 2 tablespoons butter. Grease an ovenproof dish and put in alternate layers of potato purée, onions, and ham, ending with a layer of potato purée. Sprinkle with the bread crumbs, dot with the rest of the butter, and bake for ½ hour in a moderate oven (350° F.).

POTATO SOUFFLÉ
Aardappel-soufflé

2   pounds boiled potatoes
1   cup milk or cream
3   tablespoons butter
5   egg yolks
½   teaspoon salt

⅛ teaspoon grated nutmeg
5 egg whites

6 SERVINGS

Rub the boiled potatoes through a sieve. Heat the milk or cream with the butter and mix with the potatoes. Stir in the egg yolks, salt, and nutmeg. Whip the egg whites until stiff and fold into the mixture. Grease a rather deep ovenproof dish with butter. Put the mixture inside and bake in slow oven (325° F.) for 45 minutes. Do not open the oven to take a look, or your soufflé will collapse.

POTATO RISSOLÉS
Aardappel croquetten

1   pound boiled potatoes
2   tablespoons melted butter
½   teaspoon salt
⅛   teaspoon grated nutmeg
2   egg yolks
2   egg whites, whipped stiff
1   tablespoon bread crumbs
Fat for frying

3 SERVINGS

Rub the potatoes through a sieve, blend in the melted butter, the salt, the nutmeg, and beaten yolk of 1 egg. Fold in the 2 egg whites. Shape the purée into small balls of about 1 inch. Roll in a mixture of the yolk of the second egg diluted with 2 tablespoons water, then through the bread crumbs. Fry in deep fat until brown. Drain on absorbent paper.

SPEKKIE SLA

4 pounds purée of Potatoes
1 pound escarole
1 pound fat bacon
Vinegar
Pepper

4 SERVINGS

A dish from the province of Gelderland, consisting of three quarters potato purée and one quarter finely cut raw escarole (endive), washed and well drained. Heat the purée very well and mix in the escarole at the last moment, just before serving. With this dish goes a huge cupful of fried, diced, fat smoked bacon in its melted fat. Put the Spekkie Sla on your plate, pour the fat and bacon over it, and make a little hole in the middle to pour in some vinegar. Grind some pepper over it—and, *"Smakelijk eten"* or, "Eat well."

This dish is very easy to prepare in advance and to mix at the last moment. A soup plate full for each person will easily disappear.

SAUTÉED POTATOES
Gebakken aardappelen

1 pound cold boiled potatoes
3 tablespoons butter or oil
½ teaspoon salt
Chopped parsley

3 SERVINGS

Slice the *cold* boiled potatoes. Fry the slices in butter or oil and salt in a frying pan. Serve topped with chopped parsley. This dish is always on the menu, even in the smallest restaurant, usually served with *biefstuk—filet mignon*—and salad.

POTATOES SIMMERED IN PARSLEY SAUCE
Aardappelen, gestoofd in peterselie saus

1 pound cold boiled potatoes
3 tablespoons butter
3 tablespoons flour
2 cups stock or water and milk
½ teaspoon salt
1½ tablespoons chopped parsley

3 SERVINGS

Slice the potatoes. Melt 1½ tablespoons butter, add the flour, and stir in the liquid. Add the salt. Simmer for 10 minutes, stirring well. Stir in the other 1½ tablespoons butter, and after the sauce is ready, add the parsley. Heat the sliced potatoes in this sauce.

Staphorst pancakes

DESSERTS

As a dessert we always have a sweet. Although we start the day having cheese for breakfast and having cheese again for lunch, it is not customary to have it as a savory.

Ice cream is still a luxury, but simple sweets, having as a base stale bread, macaroni, rice, etc., are eaten in large quantities. Pancakes are a favorite too. Maybe some of these recipes may appeal to you as a breakfast dish, instead of cereal, and certainly most children will like them.

BREAD DISH WITH APPLES
Broodschoteltje met appelen

2   pounds apples
½   cup sugar
18 slices stale bread
6   tablespoons butter
3   teaspoons cinnamon

6 SERVINGS

Make applesauce in the usual manner: boil or steam apples, rub through a sieve, and add the sugar. Butter the slices of bread on both sides and put them in layers with the applesauce in a greased ovenproof dish. The top layer should consist of bread. Mix the cinnamon with a little sugar, sprinkle on top, and bake in a moderate oven (325° F.) for 20 minutes.

BREAD DISH WITH RAISINS
Broodschoteltje met rozijnen

18 slices stale bread
2   cups milk
2   egg yolks
⅓   cup sugar
3   ounces raisins
3   ounces candied orange peel
½   cup brandy
2   teaspoons cinnamon
2   egg whites, stiffly beaten
1   tablespoon butter

6 SERVINGS

Soften the bread in warm milk and mash it fine. Add the egg yolks, sugar, raisins, candied orange peel, brandy, and cinnamon. Mix well. Fold in 2 beaten egg whites. Pour into a buttered ovenproof dish, dot with butter, and let rise in a moderate oven (325° F.) for ½ hour.

BREAD DISH WITH ALMONDS
(for children)
Broodschoteltje met amandelen

18 slices stale bread
2 cups milk
6 ounces almonds, blanched and finely chopped
2 egg yolks
1 cup sugar
2 egg whites, stiffly beaten
1 tablespoon butter
¼ teaspoon cinnamon

6 SERVINGS

Soften the bread in warm milk and mash it fine. Mix with the almonds, egg yolks, and sugar. Fold in the beaten egg whites. Pour into a buttered ovenproof dish. Sprinkle with the cinnamon, dot with butter, and let rise in a moderate oven (325° F.) for ½ hour.

BREAD DISH WITH ORANGES
Broodschoteltje met sinaasappels

½ pound white bread without crusts
2 cups orange juice
½ cup butter
2 egg yolks
¾ cup sugar
½ teaspoon grated lemon rind
2 egg whites, stiffly beaten

6 SERVINGS

Mash the bread fine in warm orange juice. Stir the butter until soft and fold in the egg yolks, sugar, and lemon rind. Blend these ingredients till they are very light and creamy. Mix with the bread. Fold in egg whites. Pour in a greased baking dish and let rise in a slow oven (325° F.) for about ½ hour.

BREAD OMELETTE
Broodomelet

½ pound stale bread
1 cup milk
½ teaspoon vanilla
Grated rind of ½ lemon
¼ cup sugar
4 egg yolks
4 egg whites, beaten stiff
4 tablespoons butter
Orange marmalade
2 tablespoons confectioners' sugar

6 SERVINGS

Soften the bread in warm milk and mash fine. Add the vanilla, lemon rind, and the sugar. Mix well with the egg yolks and fold in the beaten whites. Brown half of the butter in a frying pan, pour in *half* of the dough, and bake an omelette. Turn it over and brown the other side. Place on a warm dish and cover with some orange marmalade. Bake the other half of the dough in the same way. Put the second omelette on top the first and sprinkle with confectioners' sugar. This dish may be eaten cold or warm.

BREAD WITH RASPBERRY SAUCE
Turfjes met bessensap

12 slices stale bread without crusts
5 tablespoons butter
Bottle of raspberry sauce
Cinnamon
4 tablespoons sugar
1 cup heavy cream, whipped

4 SERVINGS

Sauté the slices of bread in the butter. Take a bottle of raspberry sauce—if necessary, add water or sugar— and pour some of the sauce over a layer of baked bread. Sprinkle with cinnamon and sugar. Cover with another layer of the baked slices of bread, pour some sauce over, and so forth. Let stand for a couple of hours. Decorate with whipped cream on top.

FRIED SLICES OF BREAD
Wentelteefjes

2 eggs
½ cup sugar
½ teaspoon grated lemon rind
¼ teaspoon cinnamon
1 teaspoon vanilla
2 cups milk
16 slices stale bread
6 ounces butter
Confectioners' sugar

4 SERVINGS

Beat the eggs with the sugar, lemon rind, cinnamon, and vanilla. Add the milk, slightly warmed. Arrange the slices of bread in layers in a shallow dish and pour the milk over them. Let stand for ½ hour. Fry the slices in the butter, but be careful that they don't break. Sprinkle with confectioners' sugar.

ZWIEBACK WITH RHUBARB
Beschuit met rabarber

6 zwieback
2 cups cooked Rhubarb (see Vegetables chapter)
1 teaspoon cinnamon
2 tablespoons confectioners' sugar
1 cup heavy cream, whipped

6 SERVINGS

Cover the zwieback with the rhubarb. Sprinkle with cinnamon and confectioners' sugar. Decorate with whipped cream and serve immediately.

ZWIEBACK WITH APPLE
IN THE OVEN
Appelschoteltje

1 cup milk
¼ teaspoon grated lemon rind
Pinch of salt
½ cup flour
½ cup butter
8 sour apples, peeled and sliced
10 tablespoons sugar
3 egg yolks
8 zwieback
3 egg whites, beaten stiff

6 SERVINGS

Bring the milk to the boil with the lemon rind and the salt. Mix the flour with 3 tablespoons butter and add to the milk. Stir well and blend into a thick sauce. Simmer the apples for 10 minutes with 1 tablespoon butter and 5 tablespoons sugar. Beat the rest of the butter until soft and stir in the remaining sugar. Blend into a creamy mixture. Add the egg yolks, the sauce, and the apples, and fold in the egg whites.

Crumble the zwieback. Take a greased ovenproof dish, put in a layer of the mixture, a layer of zwieback, etc., with the zwieback on top. Dot with a little butter and bake in a slow oven (325° F.) for about 45 minutes.

MACARONI WITH RAISINS
Macaroni met rozijnen

¼ pound macaroni
4 cups milk
3 tablespoons butter
Pinch of salt
¼ cup brown sugar
3 tablespoons raisins
1 tablespoon bread crumbs

4 SERVINGS

Boil the macaroni in the milk with the butter and salt for about 1 hour. Stir from time to time. Add the sugar and the raisins. Pour in a buttered dish, sprinkle with bread crumbs, and bake for ½ hour in a slow oven (325° F.).

RICE WITH RAISINS
Rijst met krenten of rozijnen

1 cup rice
3 ounces raisins
Pinch of salt

4 SERVINGS

Wash the rice, add the raisins, salt, and 3 cups water, bring to a boil, and simmer till dry.
Serve with butter and brown sugar.

MILK RICE
Rijstebrij

1 cup rice, washed and drained
6 cups milk
1 teaspoon salt
2 tablespoons butter
1 teaspoon vanilla

6 SERVINGS

Bring the rice to the boil in the milk with the salt and simmer till tender, about 40 minutes. Stir frequently. Add the butter and the vanilla and simmer for 5 minutes more.

This dish is eaten warm with sugar and cinnamon. When you eat it cold, combine it with fresh or stewed fruit or with a can of apricots.

RICE PUDDING
Rijstpudding

1 cup rice, washed and drained
2½ cups milk
Pinch of salt
4 tablespoons sugar
1 teaspoon vanilla
2 eggs, beaten
Grated rind of ½ lemon
⅓ cup raisins
1 tablespoon butter
Bread crumbs

6 SERVINGS

Bring the rice to a boil in the milk with the salt, sugar, and vanilla. Simmer till tender for about 40 minutes. Stir frequently. Take this mixture from the fire and stir in the beaten eggs, lemon rind, and raisins. Grease a baking dish and cover the bottom and sides with the bread crumbs. Pour in the rice mixture. Dot with butter and sprinkle with crumbs. Bake the pudding in a moderate oven (325° F.) for about ½ hour, until the pudding is set. Cool and unmold.

Serve with strawberry or raspberry sauce or stewed fruit.

RICE SOUP WITH FRUIT SAUCE
Rijstsoep met vruchtensaus

1   cup rice, washed and drained
Pinch of salt
¼   teaspoon finely grated lemon rind
3   ounces raisins
1½ cups strawberry or raspberry juice
¾   cup sugar

6 SERVINGS

Bring the rice to a boil in 4 cups water, salt, and lemon rind. Simmer for ½ hour. Add the raisins, fruit juice, and sugar. Simmer for 15 minutes more. May be eaten warm or cold.

BUTTERMILK CREAM
Hangop

This means "hang up," as one hangs up the buttermilk to let the superfluous liquid run off.

4 quarts buttermilk
½ cup heavy cream
Brown sugar
6 zwieback
Cinnamon

6 SERVINGS

Take a clean kitchen towel and knot the four corners together. Pour the buttermilk in this "sack" and hang this over a washbasin for 6 hours. It will then have the consistency of cream. Beat the heavy cream until stiff. Mix with the buttermilk and chill well. Eat this with lots of brown sugar, crumbled zwieback, and cinnamon to taste.

Another way is:
1½ cups sugar
1 can chopped pineapple

Mix the hangop with the sugar and add the pineapple. Chill well.

COCOA PUDDING
Chocolade pudding

3 tablespoons cocoa
⅓ cup sugar
¾ cup milk
1 teaspoon vanilla
1 tablespoon gelatine
½ cup heavy cream, whipped

4 SERVINGS

Mix the cocoa with the sugar and add a little milk. Boil the rest of the milk with the vanilla. Pour in the cocoa and stir until dissolved. Soak the gelatine in ¼ cup water. Add to the mixture, and stir until dissolved. Pour into a moist mold. Chill thoroughly. Unmold and decorate with whipped cream.

BUTTERMILK PUDDING
Karnemelk pudding

2   tablespoons gelatine
1   pound sugar
1   cup lemon juice
2½ cups buttermilk
1   cup heavy cream, whipped

8 SERVINGS

Soak the gelatine in ½ cup water and dissolve in as little hot water as possible. Dissolve the sugar in the hot lemon juice. Add these to the buttermilk. Stir well. Pour into a moist mold. Chill well. Unmold and decorate with whipped cream.

LEMON PUDDING
Citroen pudding

5   egg yolks
¾ cup brown sugar
Juice of 4 lemons
1   tablespoon gelatine
5   egg whites
Pinch of salt
1   cup heavy cream, whipped

6 SERVINGS

Beat the egg yolks with the sugar until light. Add the lemon juice and cook in a double boiler until creamy. Take this mixture from the fire. Dissolve the gelatine in 3 tablespoons warm water and stir into the mixture. Whip the egg whites with the salt until stiff and fold in the mixture. Pour into a moist mold. Chill well, unmold, and decorate with whipped cream.

BLANCMANGE
Roompudding

1   tablespoon gelatine
½   cup milk
2   cups cream
½   cup sugar
1½   teaspoons vanilla
1   cup heavy cream, whipped

8 SERVINGS

Soak and dissolve the gelatine in 3 tablespoons water. Bring the milk and the cream, the sugar and the vanilla to a boil. Stir the gelatine into this mixture. Cool. When this mixture starts to thicken, fold in the heavy cream, whipped stiff. Pour into a moist mold, chill, and unmold.

This is the basic recipe. The following ingredients may be added to the mixture before it starts to thicken.

6 broken macaroons
or ladyfingers soaked in brandy and crumbled
or ¼ cup ground almonds
or chopped candied fruits, (red and green)
or chopped dates or figs

RUM PUDDING
Rumpudding

4   eggs
½ cup sugar
½ teaspoon grated lemon rind
¾ cup rum
1   tablespoon gelatine
2   cups heavy cream

8 SERVINGS

Beat the eggs until light with the sugar and lemon rind. Thicken this mixture in a double boiler, and add the rum. Soak the gelatine in 3 tablespoons water, heat, and dissolve. Stir into the mixture and let cool. Whip the cream until stiff and fold into the mixture. Place the pudding in a moist mold, chill thoroughly, and unmold.

We'll conclude this chapter with Dutch pancakes and *flensjes*, very thin pancakes.

Pancakes are a national dish, usually baked with bacon and eaten with molasses. As they are very nourishing, they are considered a "meal in one." Use a large skillet, with a bottom approximately 9 inches wide.

PANCAKES
Pannekoeken

1½ cups bread flour
1   teapoon baking powder
½   teaspoon salt
2   eggs, beaten
1   cup milk
Oil or lard
Molasses or brown sugar

± 7 OR 8 THICK PANCAKES

Mix the flour with the baking powder and the salt. Make a hole in this mixture and pour in 2 beaten eggs. Mix well. Warm the milk and 1 cup water and add these slowly—stirring continually—to the mixture. No lumps are permitted in this batter. They are baked in oil or lard, not in butter. Pour a little oil in the skillet, and take care that the entire bottom is greased. Pour in the batter, tip the skillet, and let the batter spread out over the bottom. Bake brown on one side, turn over, and, adding a few drops of oil, bake the other side brown. Eat these with molasses or brown sugar.

With this same batter one can make "three in one" (*drie in de pan*), meaning bake 3 much smaller pancakes at the same time. Add 3 ounces of raisins to the batter and serve with sugar. Baking these goes much more quickly and they taste very well eaten cold.

PANCAKES WITH BACON
Spekpannekoeken

1¼ cups bread flour
2   eggs, beaten
2   cups milk
1   tablespoon oil
5-ounce slab smoked bacon
Molasses

6 PANCAKES

Make a hole in the flour and pour in the 2 beaten eggs. Mix well with a wooden spoon. Add the warm milk, stirring continually. Mix the oil through the batter. Cut the bacon in slices and put three or four pieces in a skillet to fry. Take care that the entire bottom of the pan is greased. Pour in the batter, tip the skillet, and let the batter spread over the bacon. Bake brown on one side, turn over, and brown the other side. These pancakes are eaten with molasses.

PANCAKES WITH APPLE
Appel pannekoeken

½ cup butter
3–4 sour apples

6 PANCAKES

Follow exactly the same procedure as in the recipe for Pancakes with Bacon, using sour apples cut in thin slices instead of bacon. Bake in butter instead of bacon fat.

FLENSJES *(very thin pancakes)*

¾ cup flour
3 eggs
Pinch of salt
2 cups milk
confectioners' sugar

24 PANCAKES

Make a hole in the flour, beat the eggs with the salt, and pour into the hole. Mix thoroughly with a wooden spoon. Add the milk in small quantities, stirring well. Heat a 6-inch skillet, put in a little lump of butter, and grease the bottom. Pour in a small quantity of batter. Tip the skillet and let the batter spread out. Brown on one side only. Sprinkle with sugar, roll up with two forks, and place on a warm dish.

There are various ways of eating these *flensjes.* If you bake them a day in advance, don't roll them up, but make layers with Custard Sauce (see below) in between. Chill well and cut before serving.

Of course *flensjes* can also be eaten with all kinds of jams and marmalade instead of sugar. With ginger they taste very well.

CUSTARD SAUCE
Custard saus

3 egg yolks
¼ cup sugar
Pinch of salt
1 cup milk
1 cup cream
1 teaspoon vanilla

ABOUT 2½ CUPFULS

Beat the egg yolks slightly. Add sugar and salt. Scald and stir in slowly the milk and cream. Place the custard over a very slow fire. Stir it constantly and take care that it does not boil. Or cook it in a double boiler. Strain and cool the custard. Add the vanilla.

As our food in the winter—such as bean soup or pancakes—is rather heavy, we like to end our meal with a fruit dish.

DRIED APPLES
Gedroogde appeltjes

1 pound dried apples, cut in slices
   or quartered
¾ cup raspberry sauce
Rind of ½ lemon
5 tablespoons sugar
Cornstarch

4 SERVINGS

Wash the apples the night before and cover well with water. Drain and add the raspberry sauce, lemon rind, sugar, and 2 cups water. Cook them gently until they are soft. Drain. Mix the cornstarch with some water (the quantity depends on the amount of juice). Add this to the juice and simmer until the syrup is thick. Remove the lemon rind. Pour over the apples and chill.

DRIED APRICOTS
Gedroogde abrikozen

1 pound dried apricots
4 cups white wine, or 2 cups wine and
    2 cups water
2 cups sugar

4 SERVINGS

Wash the apricots and soak them for 1 hour in water. Drain, add the wine and sugar, and simmer for about ½ hour. Chill.
Serve with whipped cream.

STEWED PEARS
Stoofperen

1   cup red wine
1   cup sugar
12 pears, peeled, cored, and quartered
2   sticks cinnamon
½   teaspoon grated lemon rind

8 SERVINGS

Boil 1 cup water, wine, and sugar. Drop in the fruit and cook until nearly tender. Add cinnamon and lemon rind and stew until tender.

STRAWBERRY COMPOTE
Aardbeien compote

1 pound strawberries
2 cups sugar

4 SERVINGS

Wash the strawberries and rub half the amount through a sieve. Bring the juice with the sugar to a boil. The sugar must be dissolved. Pour over the rest of the fruit and chill.

Serve with whipped cream or vanilla ice cream.

As there are so many different kinds of ice cream in America, it would be difficult to tell you something new about this subject. But I am sure that this old family recipe will amuse you.

SPICED ICE CREAM
Gekruid ijs

3 cups vanilla ice cream
3 slices stale black rye bread
2 tablespoons maraschino
½ teaspoon ground cloves
½ teaspoon cinnamon

6 SERVINGS

Let the ice cream get a little soft. Put the bread through a nut grinder. Add this with the maraschino and the spices to the ice cream. Mix well and freeze in the refrigerator.

"*Koek en Zoopie*"

BEVERAGES FOR PARTIES

Of course we have the ordinary beverages, such as tea, coffee, and cocoa. Drinking endless cups of tea and coffee keeps most people happy during the daytime. However, as their preparation is more or less the same all over the world, they do not call for special recipes. But on special occasions we have certain drinks that belong to that particular festivity and are part of the celebration. Maybe that is the reason why most of them are alcoholic to a certain degree. So it might be quite a good idea, when you are going to give a party and you want to do something special, to try out one of these.

ANISE MILK

This drink belongs to the festivity of skating, an occurrence that has not changed much through the ages. A little hut is built on the ice, usually of reeds, without a roof, but where one can find some shelter against the icy cold east wind. There is no floor either, as one keeps one's skates on, and the furniture consists of rough wooden benches round the walls. In the middle burns a little stove with a large pot of Anise Milk on top, and cups are handed round by a very old man all wrapped up in shawls, who tries to make a little money out of this enterprise. It is a lovely feeling to take off one's gloves and to warm your hands round the cup and feel this warming drink inside you. It gives you courage to go on skating for miles, or to the next *"Koek en Zoopie"*—meaning "Cook and Drink," because simple cookies are sold there too. There is no alcohol in this drink, as skating combined with liquor might lead to some very painful results.

ANISE MILK
Anijs melk

4   cups milk
1   tablespoon crushed anise seed
½ cup sugar
2   tablespoons cornstarch

4-6 SERVINGS

Scald the milk with the anise seed, add the sugar, and simmer for 5 minutes. Dissolve the cornstarch in a little water and add to the mixture. Stir and cook over a low fire until the cornstarch is cooked, about 5 minutes.

SLEMP

A spicy, non-alcoholic drink the children drink on the evening of the Sint Nicolaas Festival (see Sint Nicolaas chapter).

> Pinch of saffron
> 8 cloves
> 1 stick cinnamon
> Piece of mace
> 4 cups milk
> ½ cup sugar
> 2 tablespoons cornstarch
>
> 4-6 SERVINGS

Tie the herbs in a piece of cheesecloth and put in the milk. Scald and simmer for ½ hour. Add the sugar. Dissolve the cornstarch in a little water and add to the mixture. Stir and cook for 5 minutes more. Press the little bag with herbs between two spoons and remove.

CANDEEL

This drink belongs to a different type of festivity. It is a very old custom—although in the cities it has disappeared, it lives on among the farmers—that of showing a new baby to the friends of her (or his) mamma. It usually happens when the mother feels well enough to sit up in bed and enjoys wearing her most becoming bed jacket. The baby looks its very best in its christening robes, an old heirloom of handmade lace and bows. The friends admire the little newcomer, while eating various cakes, exchanging the latest gossip, and drinking Candeel out of special cups. Sometimes oblong in form, always highly decorated, they are now a cherished item of the antique shops. New ones are not made any more.

4 eggs
1 cup sugar
1 teaspoon grated lemon rind
Juice of 1 lemon
1 bottle white wine
1 stick cinnamon

Beat the eggs with the sugar until light, add the lemon rind and the lemon juice. Add the wine, and warm the mixture slightly, stirring well all the time with a wire whisk. The mixture is not allowed to boil. Add cinnamon.

CLARET CUP (warm)

This drink is called *Bisschop*, meaning Bishop, probably because of its red color. It is drunk on family gatherings in the winter. One must not forget that whisky is not our national drink, as it is in America and England. It is imported and very expensive. Only the upper classes drink it, and ninety per cent of the population has never tasted it. And as everybody wants to have a good time, one must invent another drink.

15 cloves
1 orange
1 lemon
1 cup sugar
1 stick cinnamon
2 bottles red wine

Stick the cloves in the orange and the lemon. Dissolve the sugar in 2 cups hot water and add these ingredients with the cinnamon to the wine. Put over a very slow fire for about ½ hour and strain.

PUNCH IMPERIAL

2 tablespoons tea
1 cup sugar
Juice of 3 lemons
Juice of 3 oranges
½ bottle rum or arrack
1 bottle white wine
½ bottle champagne

Prepare 1 cup very strong tea. Strain and dissolve the sugar, add the fruit juices and the arrack. Cool. Add the white wine, put on ice, and add the champagne just before serving.

Cold drinks are popular in the summer for garden parties, balls, and so on.

KALTE ENTE
"Cold Duck"

2 bottles Rhine wine
Rind of 1 lemon
¼ cup brandy
1 bottle champagne

Pour in a large bowl the wine, lemon rind, and the brandy. Cover and put on ice. Remove the lemon rind before serving and add the champagne. When this drink is made in large quantities, you may add a bottle of soda water.

Birthdays are celebrated more elaborately in Holland than in any other country in Europe, as we do not have name days. Family and friends come together to con-gratulate the unfortunate victim on having added an-other year to his or her age. Genever, or Dutch gin, is the popular favorite of all the drinks on those occasions, but as they are sold in bottles, I cannot give you the recipe. But another drink, very popular with the ladies, is the following one.

ADVOCATE
Advocaat

12 eggs
2   cups sugar
2   teaspoons vanilla
4 cups French brandy

Beat the eggs until light with the sugar and the vanilla. Put in a double boiler and add the brandy, but very slowly, stirring all the time with a wire whisk. Cool.

Serve in glasses with a little grated nutmeg on top, and with whipped cream. This "drink" is eaten with a spoon.

I will conclude this chapter by adding an old family recipe with the strange name of Hoppel-Poppel. What this means, I do not know—maybe it is a corruption of a French or English word—but for me it will always mean a souvenir of gay parties in bygone days.

HOPPEL-POPPEL

4 egg yolks
½ cup sugar
1 cup rum or arrack
¼ teaspoon grated nutmeg
1 cup heavy cream, whipped

Beat the egg yolks until light with the sugar, add, stirring well, the rum and the nutmeg, and fold in the whipped cream. Chill well. Like Advocate, this "drink" is eaten with a spoon. It could serve quite well as a dessert, accompanied by cakes or cookies. If you have an electric mixer, this is easy to make and worth while trying out.

A very simple version of a painting by Jan Steen.
Saint Nicolas night, painted in the second half of the
17th century. Rijksmuseum, Amsterdam.

SINT NICOLAAS
A Festival for Children

The evening of Sinterklaas, as he is called in Dutch, is the children's party of the year. It is the evening which brings joy and merriment to all Dutch families. Sinterklaas is an entirely different person from the Santa Claus who frolics around America at Christmastime, with his sledge and reindeer. This is a stately bishop, who arrives from Spain by boat, accompanied by his faithful servant, Black Peter. As the patron of children and sailors he can be traced back in Spain to the time of the Moors. Peter wears the seventeenth-century Spanish costume, with beret and white ruff.

To be able to visit every family in Holland, rich and poor alike, he rides his famous white stallion over the rooftops and dispenses his presents through the chimney. Black Peter, or *Zwarte Piet*, carries on his back a huge sackful of presents for the children who were well behaved during the past year, but a birch for the naughty ones.

Preparations start at least ten days before the big evening, and in the meantime the tension mounts: who will receive presents and praise, or for the unlucky ones, birch strokes and punishment?

During these days the children put one of their shoes —filled with bread, hay, or a carrot for Sinterklaas's horse—in front of the fireplace. Before going to bed they sing special songs which are taught to them at school. Next morning the food has gone and a little present or some sweets has taken its place. On the way to school they will tell each other, bragging, what the good saint has brought them.

On the big evening the whole family with its closest friends and children gathers to receive Sinterklaas, singing Sinterklaas songs in anticipation of the Bishop's arrival. Suddenly a knock on the door is heard and there enters the stately saint in full bishop's garb with his staff and long white beard. He is a friend or relation of the family, who knows everybody very well, but in his make-up no child could recognize him. After being welcomed by the head of the family and being seated in the best armchair, he asks his Peter for the big "Golden Book" in which everybody's good and bad deeds of the

Saint Nicolas

past year are recorded. Distributing the presents, he praises or reprimands the children and grown-ups alike. After he has left, the presents, accompanied by an amusing little rhyme making fun of the receiver's good or not-so-good side of his character, are opened.

Now that the tension created has been relieved, drink and food are distributed. The children drink Slemp and the grown-ups Claret Cup (see Beverages for Parties chapter). The sweet and solid foods consumed on this occasion are of a bewildering number and variety. People present each other with letters of chocolate up to eight inches in size, corresponding to their initials. Or with puppets made of a special tough gingerbread dough (*taai-taai*) in male and female forms, roughly resembling the jacks and queens of a pack of cards. The female of the species is called *vrijster* and the male *vrijer* (the sweetheart and the suitor). Needless to say, all this is shared and consumed on the spot. In between, there is Speculaas (see below), or Spiced Cookies, marzipan, baked fondant, nuts, etc., until later in the evening the party settles down to real business. At that time large platters are brought in with heaps of apple fritters and—the most devastating of all—the national Oliebollen or Dutch Doughnuts.

I will start to give you the recipe for Hard Fondant, made of sugar to which an essence has been added, such as strawberry essence, etc. This fondant is made in special molds in the shape of hearts (all sizes!), stars, squares, etc. Or small round ones the size of a dollar are used. As these are not available in America, one can use lids of tins, such as cigarette tins or cooky tins. The following recipe is very easy to make, and a successful one.

HARD FONDANT
Borstplaat

½ pound sugar
4   tablespoons milk or water
Flavoring essence (vanilla, pineapple, raspberry,
      etc.)
5   drops glycerine

Put the sugar and the milk or water in a small pan and bring to a boil. Let this boil until a drop of the liquid falling from a spoon makes a thread. Remove from the fire. Add a few drops of essence and stir continually (especially round the sides of the pan). Keep stirring until the mixture has lost its transparency and starts getting more solid. Stir in the glycerine. Have greased lids of tins ready, about ⅓ inch high, pour the mixture into these, and let it become solid. Unmold by putting them for 1 second in hot water.

There are various kinds of this sweet.

If you are fond of ginger:

½ teaspoon ginger powder
½ pound sugar
1   tablespoon preserved ginger, finely chopped
      with its liquid

Mix the ginger powder with the sugar and boil with 4 tablespoons water for 10 minutes. Add the chopped ginger and cook for 2 minutes more. Remove from the fire, etc. (see Hard Fondant, above).

To prepare Cream Borstplaat, use cream instead of water.

To prepare Coffee Borstplaat, use half coffee, half cream.

SPICED COOKIES
Speculaas

¼ cup shelled almonds
1 pound flour
½ pound butter
1 tablespoon milk
½ pound brown sugar
4 teaspoons baking powder
1 teaspoon salt
1 tablespoon cinnamon
1 teaspoon powdered cloves
1 teaspoon grated nutmeg
½ teaspoon pepper
½ teaspoon powder anise

Pour boiling water over the shelled almonds. Let them stand for 5 minutes. Drain and pour cold water over them. Remove the skins. Knead the other ingredients into a supple ball. Add more milk if necessary. Roll the dough with a lightly floured rolling pin until it is ¾ inch thick. Place on a greased baking sheet and cut it into fairly large pieces. Press the almonds in the dough. Preheat a 425° F. oven for 7 minutes. Reduce the heat and bake in a 325° F. oven for about 25 minutes. It should be nicely brown.

DUTCH DOUGHNUTS
Oliebollen

1½ cakes yeast
1½ cups milk
3   cups bread flour
2   eggs
2   tablespoons sugar
2   tablespoons raisins
1   tablespoon chopped candied orange peel
½   tablespoon grated lemon rind
1   teaspoon salt
Oil or fat for frying
Confectioners' sugar

Dissolve the yeast in a deep bowl in 3 tablespoons lukewarm milk. Put in another bowl the bread flour. With a wooden spoon, stir in, one by one, the eggs. Slowly add the rest of the milk. Stir until all lumps have gone. Add sugar, raisins, orange peel, and grated lemon rind. Add this mixture to the yeast. Cover with a cloth and set to rise for about 1½ hours. Add the salt. Fry in deep oil or fat (370° F.), dropping in a tablespoon of the dough at a time. Drain on absorbent paper. Sprinkle with confectioners' sugar.

APPLE FRITTERS
Appelbeignets

12 apples, peeled and cored
½ pound bread flour
About 1½ cups beer
½ teaspoon salt
Oil or fat for frying

Cut the apples crosswise into ⅓-inch slices. To make

the fritter batter, combine the flour and the beer with a few quick strokes. Stir with a wooden spoon until there are no more lumps in this mixture. Add salt. Dip the apple slices in this batter and fry them in deep oil or fat, 370° F. Drain the fritters on absorbent paper and sprinkle with confectioners' sugar.

BANANA FRITTERS
Bananen beignets

Peel and cut bananas into halves lengthwise. Prepare them in the same way as in the recipe for Apple Fritters.

PINEAPPLE FRITTERS
Ananas beignets

1 can pineapple slices

Drain the pineapple slices and follow the recipe for Apple Fritters.

Indonesian dishes

INDONESIAN DISHES

Many Dutchmen have spent part of their lives in Indonesia, and when they returned to Holland they brought with them a taste for Indonesian food. This they have not kept to themselves. It has become customary, even among people who have never been to the Far East, to eat Indonesian or Chinese food regularly.

There are many Indonesian and Chinese restaurants in Holland, not only in the larger cities but also in the smaller provincial towns. There exist countless Indonesian dishes, some of which take hours to prepare; but a few easy ones have become so popular that they can be regarded as "national dishes."

The Indonesian Nassi Goreng (fried rice) and the Sateh (broiled meat on skewers) or the Chinese loempiah (rissolés) and Bahmi can even be bought at every snack bar and lunch counter.

A book on Dutch food therefore cannot be called complete without a few recipes for Indonesian food.

NASSI GORENG

Always use cold, cooked rice for this dish.

Foolproof way to cook rice:

> 1 cup rice, rinsed 4–5 times
> 2 cups water
> Pinch of salt
> 4 SERVINGS

Bring the rice to a boil and simmer for 20 minutes. Never lift the lid of the pot, or stir. Wrap the pot in a thick layer of newspapers and put it between pillows. Let it stand for at least ½ hour. This will give you dry, crisp grains, and provide you with a handy way to keep the rice warm, if need be, for hours.

For Nassi Goreng always use *cold* rice. Cooking it the day before is the easiest and best way.

INDONESIAN FRIED RICE
Nassi goreng

2   medium-sized onions, chopped fine
2   cloves garlic, crushed
1   teaspoon red chili pepper, chopped fine
1   teaspoon salt
Oil
3   cups cooked, cold rice
½ pound roasted pork or ham
4   eggs
1   tablespoon butter

4 SERVINGS

Fry the onions with the garlic, red pepper, and salt in oil in a heavy skillet until the onions are brown. Add the rice and fry till golden brown, stirring frequently with a wooden spoon. Dice the pork or ham into small pieces and add to the rice. Fry for 5 more minutes.

Beat 4 eggs; add 1 tablespoon water. Heat the butter in a frying pan and bake an omelette. Cut into long strips. Serve the Nassi Goreng with these strips on top. Some people prefer a fried egg to the omelette.

This dish is eaten from a soup plate with a spoon and fork. A knife is never used. Beer is the drink that goes with it. Instead of pork or ham, roasted chicken or prawns/shrimps (1 cup) can be used.

As side dishes one should use:

> 2-inch pieces cucumber cut lengthwise
> Roasted peanuts
> Chutney
> Baked Bananas

BAKED BANANAS
Pisang goreng

4 bananas
2 tablespoons butter
Pinch of salt
Lemon juice

4 SERVINGS

Peel the bananas and cut in half lengthwise. Place them in a well-greased baking dish. Dot with butter and sprinkle with salt and lemon juice. Bake in a hot oven (450° F.) for 6 minutes.

CHINESE RISSOLÉS
Loempiahs

3   eggs
½ cup flour
⅔ cup water
Pinch of salt

For the stuffing:
    10 tablespoons *taugé* (bean sprouts)
    8   tablespoons fried chicken, shredded
    8   tablespoons roast pork, shredded
    2   tablespoons chopped celery stalks
        and leaves
    1   tablespoon chopped chives
    1   tablespoon soy-bean sauce
    Oil

12 RISSOLÉS

Make a light pancake batter with the eggs, flour, water, and salt. Fry twelve very thin pancakes.

For the stuffing: Mix all the ingredients together, divide into twelve parts, and put 2½ tablespoons of the mixture in the middle of each pancake. Roll the pancakes up, moisten the edges with egg white, fold, and led stand for a few minutes, till they stick together.

Fry in deep hot oil or fat until crisp and golden brown. Drain on absorbent paper.

CHINESE NOODLES
Bahmi

1½ pounds dry Chinese *mi* (noodles)
½ pound fried pork
6 tablespoons shredded leeks
4 tablespoons chopped celery stalks and leaves
2 tablespoons *taugé* (bean sprouts)
2 cups shredded Chinese cabbage
2 cloves minced garlic
1 cup shrimps or prawns
2 tablespoons soy-bean sauce
Oil

6 SERVINGS

Soak the *mi* in warm water and drain. Bring a pan of water to the boil and put in the soaked *mi*. Wait until the water is again on the boil, then turn off the heat! Leave the *mi* in the hot water until done, but don't let it get too soft. Drain.

In the meantime dice the fried pork. Fry the leeks, celery, and Chinese cabbage with the garlic in some oil.

Add a little water and the *taugé* and simmer till half done. The vegetables prepared this way taste at their best in the Bahmi. Mix the vegetables into the Bahmi, add the meat and shrimps, and season with 2 tablespoons soy-bean sauce. Reheat for a few minutes in the oven.

MEAT ON SKEWERS
Sateh

There are three different kinds of Sateh:

Chicken Sateh — Sateh ajam
Lamb Sateh   — Sateh kambing
Pork Sateh   — Sateh babi

Cut the meat or chicken in bite-size cubes, rub with salt and pepper, and let stand for 15 minutes. Thread five or six pieces onto a skewer. Baste with oil and roast in a slow oven (325° F.), turning frequently, or grill on a barbecue.

As the genuine sauces that go with the Satehs are very complicated, and require a great many Indonesian ingredients, I will give you a short-cut recipe for a sauce for the three of them.

SATEH SAUCE

4 tablespoons peanut butter
½ teaspoon crushed red chili pepper
2 teaspoons molasses
1 tablespoon soy-bean sauce
1 clove minced garlic
Few drops lemon juice

Mix the peanut butter with 8 tablespoons hot water, stir in all the other ingredients, and simmer for 5 minutes. Cover the Satehs with the hot sauce (sufficient for eight pieces) just before serving.

And last but not least:

SAMBAL OELEK

This is an Indonesian chili seasoning eaten with all Indonesian dishes to heighten their taste. Without Sambal, no dish is complete.

2 tablespoons red chili peppers,
chopped very fine
½ teaspoon salt
½ tablespoon oil
½ teaspoon lemon juice
½ teaspoon grated lemon rind

Mix all the ingredients into a paste. This can be kept for some time in a tightly closed jar for further use.

INDEX